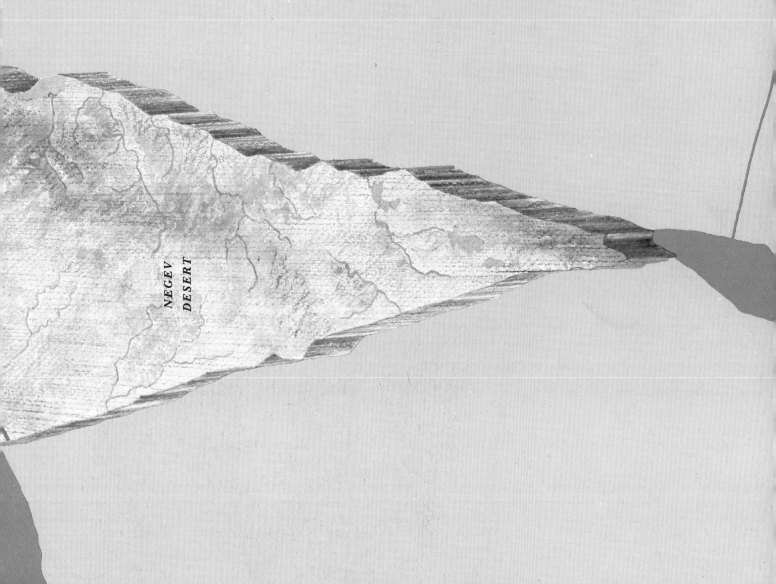

NEGEV DESERT

ISRAEL

ISRAEL

By the Editors of Time-Life Books
With photographs by Hans Wiesenhofer

TIME-LIFE BOOKS · AMSTERDAM

HOW THINGS WORK
SYSTEM EARTH
LIBRARY OF CURIOUS AND
UNUSUAL FACTS
BUILDING BLOCKS
A CHILD'S FIRST LIBRARY OF LEARNING
VOYAGE THROUGH THE UNIVERSE
THE THIRD REICH
MYSTERIES OF THE UNKNOWN
TIME-LIFE HISTORY OF THE WORLD
FITNESS, HEALTH & NUTRITION
HEALTHY HOME COOKING
UNDERSTANDING COMPUTERS
THE ENCHANTED WORLD
LIBRARY OF NATIONS
PLANET EARTH
THE GOOD COOK
THE WORLD'S WILD PLACES

TIME-LIFE BOOKS

EUROPEAN EDITOR: Ellen Phillips
Design Director: Ed Skyner
Director of Editorial Resources: Samantha Hill
Chief Sub-Editor: Ilse Gray

LIBRARY OF NATIONS

Series Editor: Tony Allan

Editorial Staff for *Israel*
Editor: Ellen Galford
Deputy Editor: Christopher Farman
Researcher: Mark Karras
Designer: Mary Staples
Sub-Editors: Sally Rowland, Frances Dixon
Picture Department: Christine Hinze, Peggy Tout
Editorial Assistant: Molly Oates

EDITORIAL PRODUCTION

Chief: Jane Hawker
Production Assistants: Nikki Allen, Alan Godwin,
Maureen Kelly
Editorial Department: Theresa John, Debra Lelliott

ISBN 0 7054 0852 3

TIME-LIFE is a trademark of Time Warner Inc. U.S.A.
D.L.TO:182-1991

CONSULTANT: Jon Kimche is the author of
many books on Israel and the Middle East. He
served for 30 years as the Middle East
correspondent for the London *Evening Standard*
and has edited a wide range of current affairs
journals and periodicals, including *Tribune,
Jewish Observer and Middle East Review, New
Middle East* and *Afro-Asian Affairs.*

Special Consultant: Professor P. J. Vatikiotis is
Professor of Near and Middle Eastern Politics at
the University of London.

PHOTOGRAPHER: Hans Wiesenhofer is an
Austrian who has travelled throughout the world
on photographic projects. He also works on
assignment for the makers of Minolta cameras as
a photographer and tutor of photographic
techniques. In addition to his assignment on
Israel, he has contributed photographs to other
volumes in the Library of Nations series,
including *France, Germany, Italy* and *Australia.*

Contributors: The chapter texts were written by:
Windsor Chorlton, William Frankel, T. R. Fyvel,
Marlin Levin and Alan Lothian. Additional
material was provided by John Laffin.

Cover: In Jerusalem's Old City, the golden Dome
of the Rock—a sacred Islamic shrine—glows
above the limestone arcades and apartment blocks
of the rebuilt Jewish Quarter. To the west, beyond
the turrets of the Roman Catholic Church of the
Dormition, new housing developments climb the
suburban hills.

Pages 1 and 2: The emblem of the state of Israel,
shown on page 1, displays a seven-branched
candlestick (*Menorah*) commemorating the
ancient Temple in Jerusalem. The candelabra is
flanked by two olive branches, linked by the name
Israel spelled out in Hebrew letters. The nation's
blue-and-white flag (*page 2*) is dominated by a six-
pointed star, the "Shield of David", an age-old
symbol first used officially as a Jewish emblem by
the Jewish community of Prague in the 1300s. The
broad blue bands, at top and bottom, represent
the stripes of the prayer shawl traditionally worn
by Jews during worship.

Front and back endpapers: A topographic map
showing the mountains, deserts and other natural
features of Israel appears on the front endpaper;
the territories occupied by Israel since 1967 are
indicated by a solid line. The back endpaper
shows the principal towns, cities and settlements.

This volume is one in a series of books describing
countries of the world—their natural resources, peoples,
histories, economies and governments.

CONTENTS

On the outskirts of the Tel Aviv conurbation, home to over one third of Israel's population, a development of solar-heated houses spreads out before an

apartment complex. Eighty-five per cent of Israelis live in the country's densely settled towns and cities.

An elderly Jewish man studies a text in Hebrew, a language written from right to left with an alphabet of 22 letters. Unlike all other modern languages,

REBIRTH OF AN ANCIENT LANGUAGE

The official language of Israel is Hebrew, a modern tongue with an ancient pedigree. Spoken by Jewish people until the third century B.C., when most of the Old Testament was written, biblical Hebrew gradually lost ground to the languages of Palestine's conquerors—the Persians, Greeks and Romans. The language survived into the 19th century only as the instrument of rabbinical study and religious ritual, its concepts and vocabulary anchoring it firmly in the world of Abraham and Moses.

In 1880, a Lithuanian Zionist named Eleizer Ben-Yehuda realized that Jews returning to Palestine needed their own language, "a language in which we can conduct the business of life". He singlehandedly began the massive task of building the Old Testament vocabulary of only 7,704 words into a contemporary vernacular. Scouring ancient texts for Hebrew roots, he adapted them to fit modern meanings. Appropriately, his first word was *millon* (dictionary), because his life's work was the completion of the first four books of a 17-volume Hebrew lexicon—the foundation of a language that now includes some 50,000 words.

Although many purists attacked him for debasing the language of worship, Ben-Yehuda's crusade succeeded. Today, Hebrew is the primary tongue of 83 per cent of Israel's Jewish population.

oken before they were written, contemporary Hebrew is the only colloquial tongue derived from a written language.

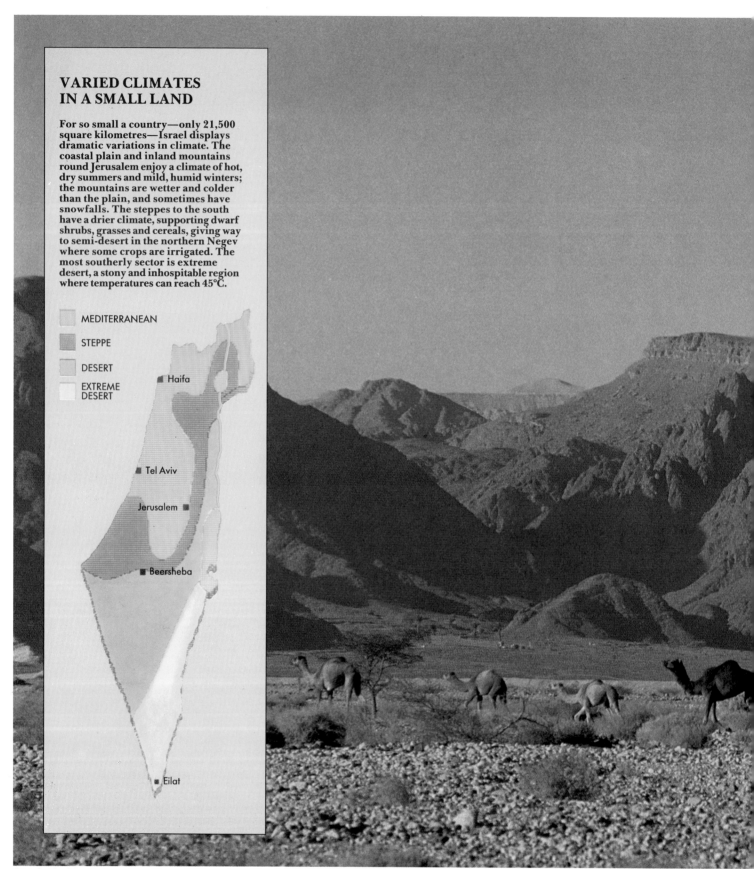

VARIED CLIMATES IN A SMALL LAND

For so small a country—only 21,500 square kilometres—Israel displays dramatic variations in climate. The coastal plain and inland mountains round Jerusalem enjoy a climate of hot, dry summers and mild, humid winters; the mountains are wetter and colder than the plain, and sometimes have snowfalls. The steppes to the south have a drier climate, supporting dwarf shrubs, grasses and cereals, giving way to semi-desert in the northern Negev where some crops are irrigated. The most southerly sector is extreme desert, a stony and inhospitable region where temperatures can reach 45°C.

MEDITERRANEAN

STEPPE

DESERT

EXTREME DESERT

Haifa

Tel Aviv

Jerusalem

Beersheba

Eilat

Overlooked by the brooding Negev Hills, a straggling herd of domesticated Arabian camels plods the stony landscape of the desert in search of edible

vegetation. Camels are superbly adapted to life in arid conditions, storing fat in their humps for nourishment when food is scarce.

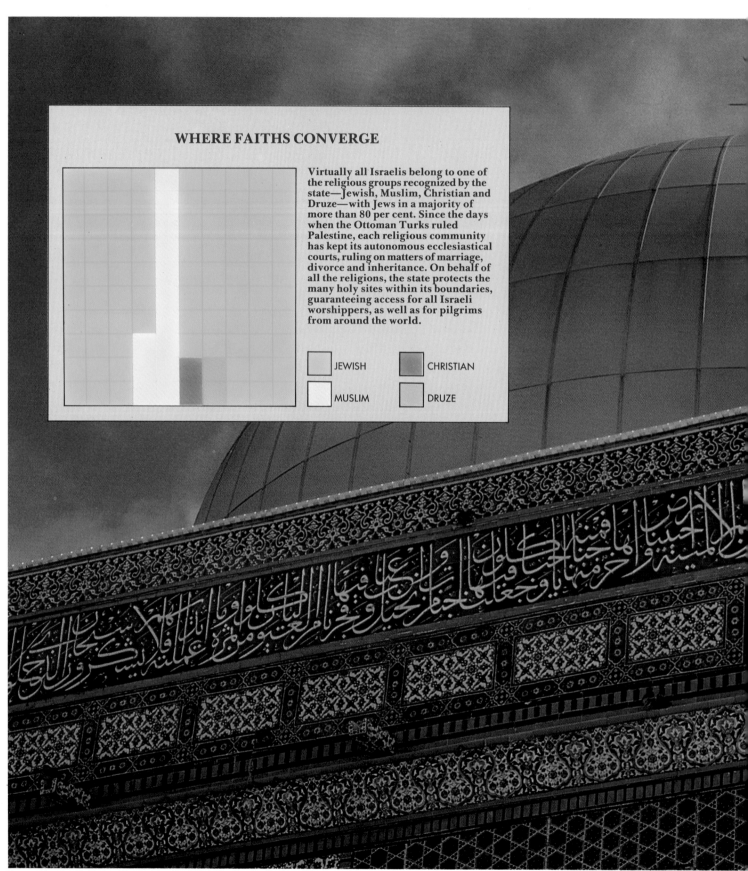

WHERE FAITHS CONVERGE

Virtually all Israelis belong to one of the religious groups recognized by the state—Jewish, Muslim, Christian and Druze—with Jews in a majority of more than 80 per cent. Since the days when the Ottoman Turks ruled Palestine, each religious community has kept its autonomous ecclesiastical courts, ruling on matters of marriage, divorce and inheritance. On behalf of all the religions, the state protects the many holy sites within its boundaries, guaranteeing access for all Israeli worshippers, as well as for pilgrims from around the world.

JEWISH   CHRISTIAN

MUSLIM   DRUZE

Raised by the Caliph of Damascus in 691 A.D., Jerusalem's gold-capped Dome of the Rock marks the stony outcropping from which Muhammad leapt to

heaven astride his miraculous horse. The rock is also sacred in Judeo-Christian tradition, as the site of Abraham's intended sacrifice of Isaac.

RECLAIMING A WASTELAND

Transformed in just four decades from hostile desert and swamp to richly productive fields and orchards, Israel's farmland is a showpiece of modern agricultural technology. The country's push for food production amidst a flood of immigration in the 1950s brought mechanization, chemical fertilizers and pesticides, and improved strains of livestock and crops to small farming settlements throughout Israel. In 1949, farmers were irrigating about 30,000 hectares; by the 1980s, the practice had spread to 220,000 hectares, in some areas producing two or more crops a year.

Although widespread irrigation revolutionized agriculture in Israel's arid zone, not all the 440,000 hectares brought under cultivation since 1930 has been reclaimed from desert. In 1951, engineers began a seven-year project to drain Lake Hula and its surrounding swamp, 60 square kilometres of malarial wasteland in Upper Galilee. By altering the course of the Jordan and constructing a network of canals, they created the country's most fertile farmland.

Today, Israeli agriculture, which employs about 82,000 people, is entirely self-sufficient in the production of vegetables, fruit, milk, eggs and poultry. Its exports range from cotton to carnations, in addition to the citrus fruits it has always marketed abroad. Israel also exports its expertise in agricultural development. Thousands of Israeli agronomists have served as consultants on irrigation and desert farming projects around the world.

A patchwork of ripening crops spreads across the broad Hula Valley, a once-desolate swampland now drained by some 40 kilometres of man-made

canals. Planted in cotton, cereals, peanuts and fruit trees, the valley is also the site of approximately half of Israel's freshwater fish ponds.

1

A STATE BORN IN STRIFE

At 4 o'clock in the afternoon of Friday May 14, 1948, shortly before the onset of the Sabbath, 200 leaders of Palestine's Jewish community gathered in the Tel Aviv Museum. After the Palestine Symphony Orchestra had played the Zionist anthem Hatikvah ("The Hope"), David Ben-Gurion rose and read out a short declaration announcing the establishment of the independent state of Israel. Twelve hours later, as the sun rose over the newborn nation, the armies of Syria, Iraq, Trans-Jordan and Egypt invaded.

Egyptian Spitfires roared over the rooftops of Tel Aviv. Radio audiences listening to a live Independence Day broadcast from Ben-Gurion could hear the thunder of bombs exploding over the outskirts of the city as he spoke. From Cairo, Azzam Pasha, Secretary-General of the Arab League warned: "This will be a war of extermination and a momentous massacre, which will be spoken of like the Mongolian massacres and the Crusades."

Few outside Israel doubted him. Although the opposing forces were roughly equal in number, the Arab armies were well-equipped with modern artillery and armour, supplied by Britain and France, while the Israelis were relying on 3-inch British/American mortars left over from World War II, old French 65-mm howitzers of the type used in the 1870 Franco-Prussian War, and kibbutz-made armoured cars. The Syrians advanced into Upper Galilee,

the Iraqis crossed the coastal plain to a point barely 15 kilometres from the sea, threatening to split Israel in two, and the Trans-Jordanian Arab Legion laid siege to Jerusalem, capturing the Old City with its Jewish quarter on May 25. In the south, one Egyptian thrust reached a point 30 kilometres from Tel Aviv, while another approached Jerusalem from the south.

But the Israelis, better-trained than their enemies and fighting for their very existence, weathered the initial attacks. Gradually, they went over to the offensive, retaking all the territory lost in the first few weeks except for the Old City of Jerusalem. As fighting continued, they took new territory, in the Galilee, Judaea and the Negev, where only the Gaza Strip, bordering the Sinai peninsula, remained in Arab hands. The war, interspersed with truces and cease-fires, continued until July 1949, when Syria signed an armistice agreement with Israel. Altogether it had cost the 600,000-strong Jewish population some 6,000 lives; the Egyptian forces lost 1,500 men, while the casualties of other Arab states are not known.

Both sides believed their cause was just. The Jews were fighting to establish an independent state in Palestine, the narrow strip of eastern Mediterranean coastline that had been the home of their ancestors in biblical times. For nearly 2,000 years they had been a scattered, persecuted people, who kept the memory of their homeland green in

Silhouetted against a sun-baked artillery range, three soldiers prepare to test their marksmanship with high-powered rifles. National defence is the first priority of the Israeli government, accounting for more than one quarter of its annual budget.

their prayers and psalms: "If I forget thee, O Jerusalem: let my right hand forget her cunning."

This longing for Zion—their ancient name for the lost holy city—became one of the bonds that kept the Jews together in the Diaspora, the places of their dispersal. Then finally, late in the 19th century, there emerged a movement of Jewish nationalists—Zionists—who sought to end the long exile and return to Palestine.

But the Arabs of the Middle East questioned this claim. Jews, they said, may have occupied the place in ages past, but Arabs had lived continuously on the land since the seventh century A.D. (Indeed, according to some Arab historians their ancestors were the original Semitic inhabitants whom the wandering Israelites supplanted.) The local Arabs themselves were never the sovereign power—Palestine had been annexed by one foreign power after another—but they had eked a living, however precariously, from the stony soil. By the beginning of this century, the Arab communities throughout the Middle East were growing restive under the domination of the Ottoman

Turkish Empire, and were gradually beginning to develop their own nationalist movements.

Inevitably, the conflicting interests and aspirations of the Arabs and the growing numbers of Zionist settlers led to strife: as the 20th century progressed, Palestine increasingly became one of the world's trouble spots. With words as well as weapons, Arabs and Jews contested the land, sowing seeds of bitterness that continue to bear fruit today.

By the 1930s, the need for a homeland was no longer only a matter of idealism, but a question of survival: Germany brought forth Hitler, and the Nazi programme for the extermination of the Jews. And while the Arabs may have watched this unfolding tragedy in Europe, they stiffened their resistance to the Zionist threat.

After the defeat of Germany, when Europe's refugee camps were crammed with 300,000 homeless Holocaust survivors, the new United Nations proposed a solution to the conflict: a partition of Palestine into separate Jewish and Arab states. Jerusalem would be designated an international city, freely accessible to the adherents of all faiths.

The proposal to internationalize the city was rejected by King Abdullah of Jordan, who occupied the Arab part of the city, and by the Jews.

Nevertheless, in November 1947, the United Nations General Assembly did vote in favour of partition, giving the Jews control of 14,245 square kilometres of the land and the Arabs 11,655 square kilometres.

On this particular issue the United States and the Soviet Union were, for once, in accord: the establishment of an independent Jewish state in the strategically vital Middle East suited both nations' political interests, and both gave their blessing.

As a result, the birth of the new country was greeted simultaneously by a fund of international good will and by implacable Arab hostility. The Arab nations saw the mass-immigration of Jews into the new state as one more manifestation of European colonialism. They felt that the West, and the U.S.S.R., were using the establishment of Israel as a way to solve Europe's post-war Jewish refugee problem (and to assuage Europe's collective post-Holocaust guilt) at Arab expense.

About 450,000 Palestinian Arabs had left the country as a result of the establishment of the Israeli state in May 1948. They sought refuge in Syria, Jordan, Lebanon and in the Gaza Strip.

Any opportunities that had arisen for the Jews and Arabs to work out some form of peaceful coexistence had been missed or mishandled by all parties. The needs and aspirations of the two peoples appeared to be irreconcilable.

Indeed, the emergence of a Jewish nation-state had a revolutionary impact on the Arab world. In Egypt—Israel's principal and most powerful Arab adversary—the resulting tremors led to the overthrow of King Farouk in 1952. The new regime of "Free Officers", headed by Gamal Abdel Nasser, promoted a militant Egyptian-directed Arab nationalism which sought to confront and constrain the emergent Jewish state. It culminated in the Sinai Campaign of 1956, when Israeli forces defeated the Egyptians in the barren peninsula between southern Israel and the Suez Canal, achieving victory after barely 100 hours of combat. Israel held all of the peninsula for six months, then withdrew after se-

curing a United Nations pledge to guard the Gaza Strip. In addition, the Egyptians undertook to allow Israeli ships passage through the Gulf of Aqaba from her new port of Eilat.

Ten years later, in June 1967, the Egyptians, along with Jordan and Syria, sought to redress the balance and set up a blockade against Israel in the Gulf of Aqaba. But, in a series of surprise manoeuvres that have been described as one of the swiftest and most shattering feats of arms in history, the Israelis were able to destroy the opposing air and ground strength in a war lasting only six days.

In this clash, Israel retook the Sinai and also acquired the Gaza Strip, the Golan Heights—the strategically important highlands between Israel and Syria—and all the Arab territories on the West Bank—the 50-kilometre-wide band of territory between Israel's 1949 eastern boundary and the Jordan River, including East Jerusalem with its Old City. For all Jews, the taking of the Old City after savage hand-to-hand fighting was the greatest triumph of the war, since it gave them access to the Western Wall, a remnant of the Second

Temple and the most sacred shrine of the Jews, from which they had been barred by the Jordanians since 1948.

This time the Israelis did not hand back the gains of war. In lieu of a final peace settlement and negotiations with the Arabs for recognized and secure boundaries, the armistice boundaries of 1949 were swept away and all the occupied areas were placed under Israeli military administration.

It was the Israelis who were taken by surprise in 1973. The Egyptians invaded the Sinai on Yom Kippur, Jewry's holiest day, reclaiming a narrow strip of the Suez fringe territory lost in the Six Day War, before they were halted by Israeli counterattacks; the fighting spilled over to the Egyptian mainland.

The Egyptians' initial success, however, helped to restore their self-confidence, making it easier for them to negotiate a peace treaty with Israel. It was finally signed in March 1979. This agreement—for which Israel's Prime Minister Begin and Egypt's President Sadat were jointly awarded the Nobel Peace Prize—was successfully implemented in April 1982, when Israel handed back the Sinai to Egypt. The

The mosques and minarets of Acre's Old City overlook its harbour—the busiest in the Holy Land until 19th-century commercial shipping outgrew it. Once a strategic prize for invading Greeks, Romans and Crusaders, Acre today is home to a small fishing fleet.

1

Peeping over a Bedouin veil, smiling beneath a chic European bob, gazing benignly above Christian vestments— the faces of Israel are a vivid mosaic of diverse peoples. The varied Semitic groups native to the Holy Land, from nomadic desert tribes to communities of Druze, live alongside newcomers from all the lands where Jews were scattered. The resettlement of entire towns from places as farflung as Yemen, Bulgaria, Iraq, Morocco and India has kept ethnic identities alive, but Israeli nationality is a common bond. Today, blue-eyed children whose Polish grandparents fled fascism in the 1930s share citizenship with black Jews from Ethiopia, Palestine Arabs, Armenians, and Baha'is of Persian descent.

1

withdrawal met with bitter opposition in some Israeli quarters—particularly among military officers who felt that the desert should be retained as a defence buffer against any future attack from the south, and among the Jewish settlers who in some cases had to be evicted by force from the lush settlement they had cultivated in the Sinai desert soil.

This new Israeli–Egyptian accord was rejected by most other Arab states, and by the Palestinian nationalist movement, whose main military and political wing, the Palestine Liberation Organization (PLO), continued to attack targets in Israel from bases inside Lebanon. On June 6, 1982, a large Israeli armoured force crossed the northern border in an invasion designated "Operation Peace for Galilee", a campaign designed to eliminate the PLO presence in the Lebanon. The Israeli bombing of Beirut and the capture of many PLO positions eventually led to the forced evacuation, by land and by sea, of some 8,000 PLO personnel. Yet the war continued against Syrian forces and Lebanese Muslim guerrillas into 1985, with losses on both sides escalating even as Israeli troops withdrew.

In spite of all the blood that has flowed, Israel and its neighbours have not as yet achieved a lasting, formal peace. The nation's boundaries remain in dispute, and the very right of Israel to exist as a sovereign state has so far not been officially acknowledged by most Arab governments.

Thus an Israeli who came young to the Promised Land may have seen combat in five wars in less than four decades. Moreover, some Israelis have fought two or three times for the same strategic point. And the battlegrounds are never more than a few hours' bus-ride from home. In so small a nation, the names recorded on the casualty lists are often those of friends or relatives. "The secret of this country," a Haifa doctor once observed, "is that there is no unknown soldier."

Inevitably, the conflicts have made their impact on the Israeli character. On the one hand, their feats of arms have given Israelis a sense of self-confidence and competence, a feeling that the long roll-call of martyrs from the days when the Jews were a persecuted, subject people is a thing of the past. On the other hand, decades of encirclement by hostile Arab neighbours have bred a claustrophobic sense of isolation, an indifference to affairs outside their own region, and a certain cynicism about the motives of other countries—even friendly ones. They know they are the focus of considerable world attention—only Washington D.C. and Paris play host to a larger foreign press corps than Jerusalem—and Israelis often feel they are judged by a harsher standard than their opponents. Yet no outside observer can be more critical of Israel than the Israelis themselves. The invasion of Lebanon, for example, stimulated a vast groundswell of dissent: many citizens questioned the validity of the war. And the establishment of Jewish settlements on the West Bank has been as contentious an issue in Israel itself as it has been outside.

In times of crisis their mood can swing violently between euphoria and depression, depending on the news they receive. Israelis are the world's most avid listeners to news broadcasts, for they know that, in the political maelstrom of the Middle East, their country's fortunes may change between one news bulletin and the next.

Even in battle they listen to the news as they make it: an estimated 70 per cent of combat soldiers in the Six Day War took their radios with them to the front.

In a country so often on the firing line, it is not surprising that there should be a conspicuous military presence. With the exception of ultra-Orthodox Jews, the medically exempt and the Arab minority, all Israelis must serve in the Zahal, the country's unified Defence Forces. Men are mobilized at the age of 18 for three years, and until they are 40 they must report for 31 days' training annually; thereafter, until the age of 55, they must serve 14 days a year. Women, who serve as drivers, instructors, communications personnel, but not as front-line combatants, are drafted for two years and are liable for the reserves up to the age of 34, or until they have a child. There is truth in the remark that an Israeli is a soldier with 10 months' annual leave.

In Israel the military are everywhere. At every major road junction there are queues of armed, hitch-hiking soldiers; road blocks guard the approaches to sensitive Arab areas; and armed sentries patrol the barbed wire fences that surround nearly all the more isolated settlements.

On the Golan Heights, the sense of a country under siege is oppressively strong. The roads are corrugated by tank tracks; the route signs are riddled by bullets fired, apparently, by advancing Syrian troops; yellow posts every 100 metres or so mark the entrance to bomb shelters. In some places, burnt-out tanks and broken-backed personnel carriers remain as fossil evidence of past wars. Buzzards perch on abandoned, shell-shattered Arab villages; gazelles step daintily across minefields.

AN AGE-OLD DREAM COME TRUE

White-painted United Nations vehicles manned by cease-fire observers bump down tracks to their heavily fortified bases. On the treeless, gently undulating land nothing moves without being seen and tracked. The commanding heights bristle with gun emplacements, listening devices, radar scanners. The air seems to hum with radio traffic.

To a traveller from a peaceful land, these sights and sounds may seem sinister, but to many Israelis they are a constant reassurance. In the border areas, the military presence has been accepted as a grim necessity.

For all its military gains, Israel remains a very small country. Its total area within the 1949 armistice lines is only 20,700 square kilometres, which makes it roughly the same size as Wales or the state of New Jersey, or, as some Israelis point out, less than 1 per cent of the area of its Arab neighbours. From the Lebanese border to Sinai it is 420 kilometres long, while its width varies between 116 and only 20 kilometres. Occupied areas of the Golan Heights, the West Bank and the Gaza Strip add another 6,924 square kilometres.

To the traveller, Israel seems much bigger than it is. The reason lies in the incredible diversity of its landscapes, which confer a sense of spaciousness much larger countries sometimes lack. Beyond the heavily urbanized and relatively undifferentiated coastal plain, the most disparate of features—mountain, desert, forest and steppe—are sometimes separated by only a few kilometres. Writers of tourist brochures are fond of claiming that, in a single day in winter, you can take an early morning run on the ski slopes of Mount Hermon in the north, and then

Flanked by troops who had just helped rout the Jordanians from East Jerusalem, a young Israeli soldier doffs his helmet at the Western (Wailing) Wall on the morning of June 7, 1967—the third day of the so-called Six Day War, in which Israel defeated the forces of Egypt, Syria and Jordan. The solemn expressions reflect the awe Jews felt at the sight of their holiest shrine, cut off for 18 years by the trenches, barbed wire and battlements that had divided the city since Israel's foundation in 1948. Eye-witness and future prime minister Itzhak Rabin described the liberation's effect on battle-hardened soldiers: "Their eyes were moist with tears, their speech incoherent. The overwhelming desire was to touch the Wall...".

1

drive south in time for an evening swim among coral reefs and tropical fish in the Red Sea at Eilat. Along the way you would have passed through the sub-tropical Jordan Valley, lush with date palms and banana groves; dropped down into the valley of the Dead Sea, the lowest point on the earth's surface; and crossed the wastes of the Negev Desert, parts of which receive less than 2 centimetres of rain a year.

Given the state of Israel's roads—adequate, but hardly expressways—a safer proposal would be to take a week over the journey, which would allow you to see the fertile valleys and the forested hills of Galilee, the rolling steppelands of Samaria, and the semi-arid badlands of Judaea.

The variety of Israel's landscapes is related both to the country's abrupt changes of relief and to the fact that it lies in a transitional zone between a Mediterranean and a desert climate and is located at a crossroads between Asia, Africa and Europe. All these factors combine to give Israel a range of plant and animal life that is extraordinarily rich and varied. More than 3,000 plants and about 80 species of mammals—including hyenas, jackals, desert wolves and wild boar—are known. In terms of its natural history, Israel is a microcosm of three continents.

For different reasons, the same can be said of its human population. By virtue of its location on the cusp of Africa and Asia, at a point where ancient trade routes converge, Israel has always been a meeting place for different tribes and races, but the country's present mix of populations only began to take shape after the birth of the state, when Israel's doors were dramatically opened to Jewish immigrants from all over the world.

At the beginning of 1948, when Independence was declared, the Jewish population of Palestine was estimated to be 600,000. The non-Jewish population for the whole of Palestine on the eve of the War of Independence was about 1,800,000. The war dramatically changed the demographic balance. The mainly Arab areas of Palestine—the West Bank and Gaza Strip, with an Arab population of over a million—were annexed by Jordan and Egypt respectively. By 1951 the Jewish state of Israel had a Jewish population which had increased threefold in the three years since Independence. The Arab population of Israel, which now excluded the West Bank and Gaza, had shrunk to 165,000.

The Declaration of Independence had declared that Israel "will be open to the immigration of Jews from all countries of their dispersion", and during the war itself, 119,000 arrived, some of them becoming Israeli citizens and casualties on the same day. Most of the early immigrants were survivors of the Holocaust, but after the war, which jeopardized the safety of Jews living in Arab countries, an increasing number of immigrants came from North Africa and the Middle East.

In 1950, for example, the entire community of 50,000 Yemeni Jews was transferred to Israel by the airborne operation "Magic Carpet", and in the following year, the entire Iraqi Jewish community—numbering some 150,000 people—was brought to Israel.

Israel's total population is now in the region of 4,300,000. This figure does not include the people without Israeli

BORDERS CHANGED BY WAR

In 1947, the United Nations ratified the creation of a Jewish state in part of Palestine. Since then, successive wars have changed the boundaries of Israel. The 1949 borders marked the battle lines at the end of Israel's War of Independence with neighbouring Arab states. The 1967 Six Day War brought the Sinai peninsula, the Gaza Strip, the West Bank, East Jerusalem and the Golan Heights under Israeli control. The 1973 war with Egypt and Syria ended in Israel's withdrawal from the western bank of the Suez Canal. Israel held captured Syrian territory east of the Golan Heights until 1974, however, when the United Nations made the area a demilitarized zone. In 1979, a treaty with Egypt led to Israel's gradual withdrawal from Sinai.

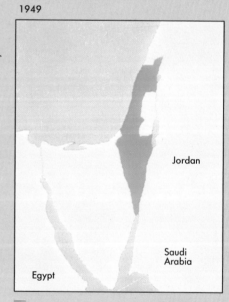

1949

Jordan

Saudi Arabia

Egypt

■ ISRAEL

ISRAELI-OCCUPIED TERRITORY

■ DEMILITARIZED ZONE

citizenship—almost all Arabs—living in the occupied zones. Eighty-three per cent of Israeli citizens are Jews, of whom just under 60 per cent have been born in the country, 22 per cent were born in Europe (including the Soviet Union) and America, and 10 per cent were born in North Africa.

During 2,000 years in the Diaspora, several different Jewish communities have emerged, each reflecting the varied cultural and linguistic conditions of the countries in which they lived. By tradition, the Jews fall into two main groups—the Ashkenazim and the Sephardim. The Ashkenazim originate from central and eastern Europe, where they spoke Yiddish or German. The Sephardim trace their origins to the culturally and materially rich Jewish community that lived in Spain until the end of the 15th century; they spoke a Spanish dialect called Ladino. Some of their followers arrived in Palestine in the 18th century where they made the northern town of Safed a centre of Jewish mysticism. Today, the Sephardim and the Oriental Jews of North Africa and the Middle East, who speak Hebrew with the same accent and follow similar religious rites, are classed together as a single religious and cultural community.

For 60 per cent of Israel's population, the mother tongue is Hebrew—a language that had been preserved primarily for liturgical and literary purposes during the Jews' two millennia of wandering. But late in the 19th century, Zionists began to adapt it for modern life in their hoped-for homeland, altering the original alphabet and vastly expanding the vocabulary.

Arabic is Israel's second official language, spoken not only by Arabs, but by a growing number of Jews, and English is the *lingua franca* and a compulsory subject at school: all three languages appear on many road signs. Though Hebrew is now the dominant form of communication, the babel of tongues resulting from mass immigration has not yet died out. Of the 23 daily local newspapers on sale in Israel in the mid-1980s, less than half were in Hebrew, with 12 of them published in Arabic, English, French, Bulgarian, Hungarian and other languages.

Israel's Muslims belong mainly to the Sunni sect, like the majority of the Arab population in the Middle East. In religious matters they enjoy virtual auton-

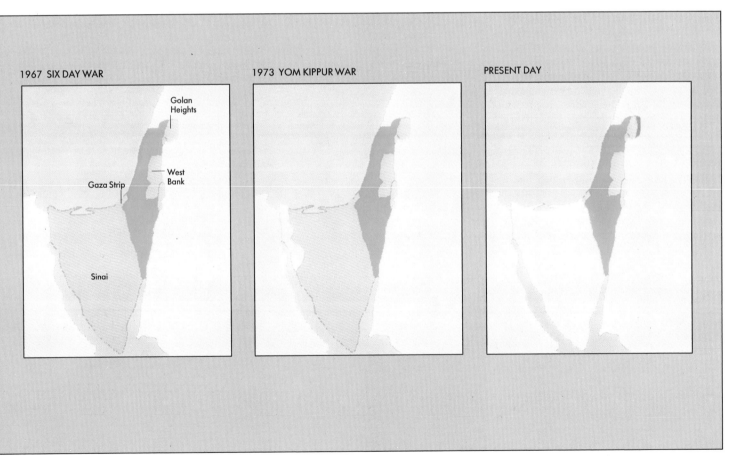

1967 SIX DAY WAR

Golan
Heights

Gaza Strip

West
Bank

Sinai

1973 YOM KIPPUR WAR

PRESENT DAY

omy, and officially they enjoy the same civic freedoms and rights as Jewish citizens of the state. They are, however, exempt from army service—not because they are under any cloud of suspicion, say Israeli authorities, but in recognition of the impossible situation that would confront them if asked to do battle against their co-religionists.

Most of the Arabs in Israel live in the Galilee, in Nazareth, or in the Haifa and Jerusalem areas, and work in the cities, where they are joined by about 35,000 workers who commute daily from the Gaza Strip. But approximately 40,000 Arabs, belonging to 23 Bedouin tribes, live in the Negev, where some of them still practise a nomadic way of life.

The Muslim population also includes about 2,500 Circassians—Sunni Muslims who came to Palestine, parts of Trans-Jordan and Syria in the 1870s, when their homeland in the Caucasus region was occupied by Christian tsarist Russia. In Israel they live in two villages in Galilee.

The Druze, of whom there were about 47,000 in the 1980s, form another religious community, with its own spiritual leadership and religious courts of law. They are the followers of a sect that grew out of Islam in the early 11th century. In the War of Independence, the Druze chose to remain in Israel, and, since 1957, the Druze youth has done military service in the Israeli Defence Forces.

About 14 per cent of the non-Jewish population in Israel are Christians; they are mostly Arabic-speaking and were born in the country. Greek Catholics account for 40 per cent of the total and Greek Orthodox for a further 30 per cent or more, but in all at least 30 denominations are represented, in-

A road to Eilat slices through the forbidding wilderness of the Negev. The scene's emptiness is deceptive: the region's wealth of minerals, ceramic clays and sand for glass-making has drawn thousands of workers to new towns developed around the mining and processing industries.

cluding Copts, members of the Syrian Orthodox, Armenian Orthodox, Roman Catholic and Ethiopian Churches, as well as various Protestant sects.

For Muslims, Christians and Jews alike, the land of Israel is holy ground: the place names are familiar throughout the world. In the north are the hills of Galilee, bounded in the east by the River Jordan. Their slopes merge with the highlands of Samaria, the ancient centre of the Samaritan sect and today a centre of militant Palestine Arab nationalism. From the hills of Jerusalem, half-way down the length of Israel, you can look south towards Bethlehem, birthplace of Jesus, or south and east to the wilderness of Judaea, where John the Baptist preached repentance and promised that "the Kingdom of Heaven is at hand". Where the Judaean hills end in the south, the Negev begins; it is here—where modern Israelis are reclaiming the desert—that the three Old Testament patriarchs, Abraham, Isaac and Jacob, pastured their flocks near the town of Beersheba.

So much history saturates the land that whenever a ditch is dug, or the foundations for a building excavated, the shovels are likely to bring up relics of long-vanished eras. Israelis are profoundly conscious of their past; indeed, they are obsessed with recovering evidence of it, as if digging down through strata of civilization's debris will put them back in touch with their origins. In Israel, archaeology is not only an important university discipline, it is also a national pastime—one that receives the kind of media coverage which other countries more usually accord to football.

It would be wrong, however, to think that the Israelis preserve their land as some kind of museum. The face of modern Israel is conspicuously new—disappointingly utilitarian, perhaps, for visitors whose imagination has been coloured by centuries of paintings depicting biblical scenes against a background of idealized landscapes. But many Israelis would defend themselves against such criticism by replying that they have had no time for romanticism: they have been far too busy fighting for their lives with one hand while building a country with the other.

When David Ben-Gurion, Israel's first prime minister, arrived in Palestine in 1906, the coastal plain he had to cross on his way to Jerusalem was largely a wilderness, its rivers lost in malarial swamps, its ancient cities in collapse and invaded by drifting sand dunes, its soil choked with weeds. A few decades later, the coastal strip between Haifa and Gaza has become Israel's most populous and intensively cultivated region, with every piece of ground outside the cities given over to citrus groves, orchards, vineyards, cotton plantations and vegetable plots.

With its regimented plantations of orange trees and their associated canneries, its hectares of vegetables shrouded in plastic sheeting and its bleak concrete dairies and chicken farms, the area is not exactly a rural idyll, but it is certainly productive. Despite a nearly sixfold population increase since 1948, by the mid-1980s the country was entirely self-sufficient in vegetables, citrus and sub-tropical fruit, milk and eggs.

The basis of Israeli agriculture was established by Zionist pioneers, who fervently believed that the salvation of the Jews was to be found on the soil. The key to its present success, however, has been the introduction of new crops,

1

new methods and, above all, the efficient exploitation of the country's meagre water resources. In Israel almost all rain falls in winter, and the average annual rainfall drops from 70 centimetres in the north to less than 20 centimetres throughout the southern half of the country. Of the 440,000 hectares under cultivation in the middle of the 1980s half were watered artificially. Some of this water comes from deep wells on the spot, but most has its source in the Jordan Rift Valley. The River Jordan may still be sacred and eternal, but only in memory. To the Israelis it is a necessary resource to be diverted, channelled, piped, made to flow uphill and generally exploited for the good of the nation.

At some points along its 360 kilometre-course, the Jordan is scarcely more than a narrow, ambling streamlet, but south of the fertile Hula Valley, reclaimed from swampland, the Jordan

justifies its name, which means "down rusher", by dropping 270 metres in 14.5 kilometres before entering the Sea of Galilee. This sea—technically a lake—is called *Kinneret* in Hebrew because, seen from afar, it resembles a harp, *kinnor*. At 213 metres below sea level, it is the lowest body of fresh water in the world. "Fresh" is something of an exaggeration, however: mineral springs, which can be seen erupting at various parts of the lake, make it noticeably saline. To Christians, it is a site of sacred memory. Here Jesus walked on the waters; here he gathered together his disciples, Simon, Andrew, James and John. And despite the changes that have been wrought—the concrete and glass hotels of Tiberias, the waterfront restaurants selling St. Peter's fish and Coca Cola, the sailboards skimming the surface—it is a place that still evokes its biblical past.

With an area of 165 square kilo-

metres and a maximum depth of 46 metres, it is also the largest reservoir, containing nearly twice as much fresh water as Israel consumes in a single year. Unfortunately, it is in the wrong place: not only does it lie well below most of the cultivated land in the country, but it is also cut off from the thirsty south by the Judaean highlands.

But, with no other suitable sources of water available, the Israelis have had to use the Sea of Galilee as the source of the National Water Carrier, a massive development project that was completed in 1964. From the north-west corner of the lake, water is pumped to a height of 256 metres and then runs in a 16-kilometre canal to another pumping station, which in turn raises it 147 metres above sea level. The water is then conducted through a series of giant pipes, aqueducts, tunnels, reservoirs and dams, which take it a maximum distance of 142.5 kilometres, across the hills of Galilee, down the coastal plain, and into the northern Negev south-west of Beersheba.

For Ben-Gurion, the completion of the project, which increased the water supply to the Negev by 75 per cent, was a major step towards the fulfilment of a long-cherished dream to make the desert bloom. The Prime Minister had described the southern desert as "Israel's greatest hope for the future", and declared that "Just as the Negev contains hidden resources, so does man; but it is in the Negev that man can become conscious of his hidden powers, arousing him to tap them and put them to creative use."

Ben-Gurion's passionate attachment to the desert was rooted in practical concerns: with an area of 14,000 square kilometres, the Negev made up about 65 per cent of the new state, forming a

On a wildlife reserve in the Negev, where conservationists are attempting to re-establish the flora and fauna native to the ancient Holy Land, a herd of rare scimitar-horned oryx rest beneath a shady acacia tree. Israel has some 180 nature preserves.

natural buffer defence zone and a vital link to the Red Sea and the countries beyond the Indian Ocean. Here, he believed, was the vital living space for Israel's future immigrant population and for its anticipated factories and towns.

Yet at the inception of Israel's statehood, the Negev was largely *terra incognita*—a weird desolation of sand and scrub, bare rock striated with lurid colours, chasms, canyons and strange craters, mountains carved into fantas-

tic shapes. The heat sits on the land like a weight, and sometimes a blistering east wind—the *khamsin*—blows for days on end, dry as a furnace, making any activity, even sleep, difficult. Buried under the sands of the desert are the ruined cities of Nabateans and Byzantines, whose inhabitants succeeded in cultivating parts of the Negev during the first millennium A.D.

But in 1948 the only town in the Negev was Beersheba, with 3,000 inhabi-

tants—a market place for the 15,000 Bedouin grazing their flocks in the region, and a rough-and-ready frontier post for the farmers of 27 Jewish villages, whose fields were supplied with water from 200 kilometres of firehoses that had last seen service in the London Blitz. There were no proper roads; when Israeli forces mounted an attack on the Egyptian army during the War of Independence, they had to hastily excavate a sand-covered Roman road

During the pecan harvest in the Galilee, a small boy watches brightly dressed Arab women gather nuts for a co-operative Jewish farming settlement. Arabs provide about half the hired agricultural labour in Israel.

1

known only to a few archaeologists, including Yigael Yadin, at that time Chief of Operations of the Israeli Defence Forces. And, apart from the presence of potash, there were no known natural resources.

However, Ben-Gurion's belief in the Negev has been vindicated. By the mid-1980s, the population of the area had soared to about 230,000, including some 40,000 Bedouin, most of whom had abandoned their nomadic way of life. Some 100,000 people live in Beersheba, the hub of development in the Negev. Roads radiate from it like spokes, linking a necklace of new towns to the north, cutting south across the desert to Eilat, running east to the Dead Sea and west to the new port of Ashdod. Around Beersheba, a green carpet, ragged and incomplete in parts, unrolls over the desert—57,000 hectares of irrigated farmland which supports 55,000 people and produces all the vegetables, dairy products and fruit consumed in the Negev.

But not even the National Water Carrier can make the entire desert bloom. And although Israel uses more than 90 per cent of all its available water resources, that is sufficient to irrigate only 41 per cent of the country's potential farmland, which is why plans are going ahead to produce fresh water from the Mediterranean sea. In the meantime, the bulk of the Negev's wealth comes from minerals—copper ore from Timna, near Eilat; kaolite from Maktesh Ramon, a giant crater in the middle of the desert; and methane gas from the Zohar fields in the northern Negev.

The real mineral treasure chest, though, lying north-east of the Negev, is the Dead Sea, a 76-kilometre-long turquoise ribbon nestling 398 metres below sea level between the biscuit-coloured mountains of Jordan and the abrupt, precipitous eastern edge of Judaea. Here all the waters of the Jordan that do not get diverted into the National Water Carrier reach journey's end, to be evaporated by temperatures that commonly reach 40°C between May and August. Despite the forbidding name, there is life in this eerily beautiful place: date palms, vegetables and grains are grown at the oasis of En Gedi, next to a nature reserve which is the last stronghold of a small population of leopards and a thriving herd of Nubian ibex. Tourist coaches ply the western shore, ferrying passengers in air-conditioned comfort to Masada, the imposing clifftop fortress where 960 Jewish zealots chose to kill themselves rather than submit to Roman slavery, and to Qumran, the site where in 1947 a young Bedouin stumbled on the ancient Judaic documents known as the Dead Sea Scrolls.

The sea itself is utterly lifeless, for the slow accumulation of minerals brought down by the Jordan and the wadis of Judaea have made its water 10 times saltier than the Mediterranean—salty enough, as everyone knows, to force even a non-swimmer with suicidal intentions to float effortlessly on its surface. The mineral content of the sea is staggering: 22 billion tonnes of magnesium chloride, 12 billion tonnes of common salt, six billion tonnes of calcium chloride, a billion tonnes of magnesium bromide, plus significant quantities of sulphates, caesium, cobalt, lithium, rubidium and manganese.

Tourists pay large sums of money to stay in spa hotels where they can immerse themselves in this chemical soup or coat themselves with sulphurous Dead Sea mud. Medical evidence is fairly conclusive that the effects are beneficial. But the serious business of exploiting the Dead Sea's resources takes place at its southern end, at the Dead Sea Works, close to the spot where God rained fire and brimstone on Sodom and Gomorrah, and where Lot's wife was turned into a pillar of salt. The sites where the Cities of the Plain probably stood are now covered by glittering mineral flats, criss-crossed by an intricate system of dykes and evaporation pans.

Ben-Gurion was able to observe the transformation of the desert at first hand, having left office in 1953 and joined an agricultural settlement which he had helped found at Sede Boker, 51 kilometres south of Beersheba. Fourteen months later he resumed political office, first as Minister of Defence and then again as Prime Minister, but in 1963, at the age of 77, he returned to Sede Boker and remained there until his death in 1973.

Sede Boker is a typical example of that most distinctive, most venerated and most adventurous of Israeli institutions—the kibbutz, an agricultural settlement in which all property is owned in common and all decisions are taken collectively. The first kibbutz was established in 1909 by early Zionist immigrants to Palestine at Degania, on the Sea of Galilee. Now there are about 270 kibbutzim, each embodying a simple principle: from each according to his abilities, to each according to his needs. Their structure is based on equality in everything: work, housing, food, clothing and childcare.

In the early days, the kibbutzim were spartan outposts of Jewish settlement, and their place in the annals of the country was earned by land recla-

mation, swamp drainage, malaria eradication and guarding of the country's borders. All their income came from agriculture, and the land was worked only by their members. Today, however, a typical kibbutz is virtually a garden suburb with spacious lawns, air-conditioned houses, a swimming pool, library, gymnasium and often even a beauty salon.

Agriculture is still a major occupation; in the mid-1980s, the 100,000 or so kibbutzniks cultivated 42 per cent of the available land and produced half of all its agricultural output. But most of the revenue comes from kibbutz industries, workshops and guest houses, and much of the farm work is now done by

hired hands, often Arabs from the nearby villages, or foreign volunteers on short-term visits.

To be a member of a kibbutz is to belong to an élite: not only do kibbutzniks enjoy the best living conditions in the country, they can also look forward to obtaining the best jobs. And although they make up barely 3 per cent of the population, they exert an influence out of all proportion to their numbers. The kibbutzim movement has counted amongst its members three of Israel's first six prime ministers; between 1949 and 1967, about a third of all cabinet ministers were kibbutz members; and in the Six Day War, 30 per cent of the country's air force pilots and 22 per

cent of the army officers were the products of the kibbutz system. Privilege has its price, however; of the 778 fatal casualties sustained by Israel in the Six Day War, 200 were from kibbutzim.

Although in theory membership of a kibbutz is open to any Israeli, there is no rush to join the ranks. Even at the beginning of the kibbutz movement, 40 years before the establishment of the Jewish state, many settlers found the socialist principles too rigorous and the communal existence too stifling. In 1921 some of them broke away to form a moshav, the prototype for another Israeli experiment in collective living.

A moshav is a co-operative agricultural settlement in which each farmer

31

1

Adrift in the Dead Sea—actually a lake at the earth's lowest point below sea level—a lone bather floats effortlessly in water with a salt content of 25 per cent. Rapid evaporation in the hot climate causes both the high salinity and the perpetual haze that veils the Jordanian hills on the far shore.

owns his own home and works his own plot of land, receiving any profit it may yield. All produce is marketed through the co-operative, which also helps its members to buy seed, fertilizer and fodder, and to obtain credit. It maintains machinery and vehicles, workshops and stores, and erects and maintains public installations such as irrigation plants, dairies, schools and clinics. After Independence, attempts were made to settle immigrants from widely different backgrounds—such as Romanian and Moroccan Jews—in a single moshav. Community resistance proved so strong, though, that the policy now is to house only a single ethnic group, or a number of similar ones, on any one settlement. At the beginning of the 1980s there were about 350 moshavim with a population of some 130,000.

While the concept of the moshav has been imitated in Africa, Asia and in some of the Latin American countries, the kibbutz has caught the imagination of the world without stimulating the world to emulate it. Even among kibbutz members of the third or fourth generation, there are worries that the movement is anachronistic, stifling and ideologically compromised.

Outsiders often imagine that the typical Israeli is a kibbutznik, but 85 per cent of the population live in cities and towns. While Israel is best known for its military exploits and pioneering agriculture—both, significantly, areas often closed to Jews of the Diaspora— the development of its urban centres has scarcely been less impressive.

Consider Tel Aviv, Israel's largest city. When Ben-Gurion landed in Palestine it did not exist; the site where it now stands was a bleak expanse of sand dunes north of Jaffa, one of the world's oldest ports: Jonah was said to have sailed from here to meet his destiny with the whale, and it was also here that the Lebanese cedar wood for King Solomon's Temple was landed on its way to Jerusalem.

Tel Aviv's early history is less romantic. It was founded in 1909 by two societies set up by Jaffa Jews, who chose the site for a suburb simply because plots were offered there at a reasonable price. Nobody imagined that it would grow into a city; for one thing, the climate is thoroughly unpleasant, oppressively humid in summer and wet and windy in winter. The impetus for Tel Aviv's rapid growth was provided by the wave of immigration that followed World War I.

In 1921, when its population was about 13,000, it was granted municipal status—the first all-Jewish city in modern history. By 1925, the population had risen to 34,000, and Tel Aviv boasted the first Jewish theatres and the first Jewish secondary school. Its population had risen to 120,000 by 1935, making it the largest urban centre in Palestine. In 1936, the port of Jaffa was closed down and a new port was built in Tel Aviv. In 1950, Jaffa was combined with its former suburb to become Tel Aviv-Yafo, the Hebrew version of its old Arab name, Yafa. The ugly duckling had taken over the nest.

Independence and the establishment of Jerusalem as the nation's capital did not halt Tel Aviv's growth. Although the seat of government was transferred, many of the government offices remained in Tel Aviv, along with the headquarters of the main political parties and the offices of all the national newspapers except for the *Jerusalem Post*. By the mid-1980s, more than 1,555,000 people—almost a third

1

of Israel's population—lived in the metropolitan area of Tel Aviv. Nearly half of Tel Aviv's workers daily commuted from outside the city, helping to jam the city's streets during the rush hour with about half of all the vehicles in the entire state.

As well as being Israel's commercial heart, Tel Aviv is the country's cultural and social centre. Two of Israel's seven universities—an extraordinary number for a country with a population barely more than half that of London or New York City—are in Tel Aviv. About three quarters of Israel's 100 or so publishing houses are based in the city and they produce about 2,000 titles a year, giving Israel the second-highest per capita book production in the world (Switzerland is the highest). Tel Aviv also boasts dozens of art galleries, six theatrical companies and three concert halls, including the Mann Auditorium, home of the internationally renowned Israel Philharmonic Orchestra, which has a subscription list of 36,000 patrons—more supporters, per head of population, than any other orchestra in the world. For informal entertainment, there are innumerable cafés and, of course, the beach.

Tel Aviv is not a beautiful city. Apart from the inevitable multi-storey hotel and office blocks and a few outposts of individuality such as the Eastern European-inspired houses in the "old" centre, the conurbation is an ungainly sprawl of four or five-storey, prefabricated concrete apartment complexes. When you have seen one, you have seen the lot, and unfortunately, the same uninspired design is to be seen in almost every city in Israel.

The ruthless standardization of housing was forced on the government as the only means of providing homes

for the immigrants who flooded into Israel after Independence. In 1949 there were more than 100,000 Israelis living under canvas in temporary camps, and thousands more Israelis were arriving every week. Yet within a decade, the camps had been cleared, and between 1948 and 1970, nearly 700,000 homes had been completed, making Israel's rate of house construction the highest recorded for any nation in proportion to its population. At the time of construction, these houses were modern and well-equipped by the standards of the region, with the majority fitted with baths and inside toilets. But the speed and cheapness of their construction meant that the quality was frequently shoddy, and many housing developments less than 30 years old have subsequently been condemned as slums and demolished.

Since the 1960s, the quality of government-financed housing has improved. Successful attempts have also been made to divert new immigrants away from the main urban centres to new towns which, though still resolutely medium-rise, have won praise for their imaginative planning and attractive landscaping. Typical of these modern developments is Ashdod, a town of about 60,000 people situated 40 kilometres down the coast from Tel Aviv. It was built from scratch in 1959 as a deep-water port. And by 1966 Ashdod had made Tel Aviv's own facilities redundant, only 30 years after that city had itself usurped Jaffa's position as chief port of the region. The pace of development and change in Israel is bewilderingly swift.

In development towns as well as in the large cities, most Israelis live in housing that is co-operatively owned and

34

managed by their residents. The system is characteristically Israeli, nurturing a degree of neighbourliness that is rare in other countries. Even more neighbourly are the *shikunim*—planned developments built for people who already know each other, and who are usually members of the same ethnic groups or professions, or even belong to the same political parties. Thus there are *shikunim* for Polish Jews, journalists and Zionist veterans.

You can see these *shikunim* on the outskirts of Jerusalem, where the architecture of utility has combined with the politics of expediency to transform the setting of one of the most ancient cities on earth. For 4,000 years Jerusalem stood alone in a natural theatre of hills, commanding views across the Judaean wilderness, where prophets communed with God, and beyond to the Hills of Moab across the Dead Sea, where Moses first gazed on the Promised Land. This outlook hardly changed until 1948, when the Israelis erected all the trappings of a modern capital—public agencies, ministries and parliamentary buildings—to the west of the Old City. Since 1967, when the Old City was annexed by Israel, its horizons to the north and west have been blocked with apartment houses hastily built for the influx of Jews. The population, which was only 160,000 at the time of Independence, has now risen to more than 750,000.

Jerusalem still contrives to remain visually bewitching. Partly it is an effect of the topography, broken by many open spaces, which lends interest to even the most mundane of modern developments. Partly it is an effect of the local stone, which is still used for the façades of most buildings—a creamy pink limestone that seems to give out its own luminescence in the clear, high air. And then there is the Old City, standing on the ruins of its own past and separated from the present by a 400-year-old Turkish wall that encloses 4 square kilometres of vaulted alleys, synagogues, mosques, churches, monasteries and convents.

Jerusalem has few of the assets which usually determine the growth of a great city. It is perched on the crests of the Judaean hills at an altitude varying between 600 and 800 metres, and its setting not only makes it cold in winter but for most of its history has rendered it difficult of access. It has no agricultural hinterland, no traditional industries, not even an adequate water supply. Its single great resource, and its outstanding asset, is its holiness, which is based on a simple and universal principle: One God.

The whole of the Old City of Jerusalem is a monument to this idea, but the bloody history of these few hectares and the division of the city into Moslem, Armenian, Christian and Jewish quarters is evidence that the simpler and more universal the idea, the more controversial it may prove to be. The pioneering Zionists saw this when they drew up a blueprint for a society in which religion would have little part.

Even in 1967 the annexation of East Jerusalem was defended on patriotic as well as religious grounds. Its remnant of the ancient temple's Western Wall was, for the vast majority of Israelis, a symbol of national regeneration rather than a religious shrine. When they touched it for the first time, they touched the keystone of 4,000 years of history, a tangible link with the origins of a people who had nothing but their collective memory to sustain them during the centuries of wandering.

Prayers finished, a young worshipper strides purposefully away from the Western Wall. A stop at Judaism's holiest shrine fits as neatly into his day as the white prayer shawl tucks under the collar of his sombre business suit.

Hardy goats forage on the desert hillsides of the Negev, as they have done ever since Abraham's time, some 4,000 years ago.

THE LANDSCAPES OF THE BIBLE

The Bible has for centuries been at the very core of Christian and Jewish thought, giving the names and places of the Holy Land a symbolic significance the world over. The legends of the patriarchs, the searing words of the prophets and the chronicles of the gospel writers have made such names as the Jordan and Jerusalem, Galilee and Jericho, Nazareth and Bethlehem universally familiar, yet dissociated from the concrete reality of any particular mountains, rivers, deserts and towns.

In Israel, such names belong to real places. Archaeology and scholarship have amplified the accounts of the Old and New Testaments, so that everywhere in this ancient country the present recalls the past. Far back in the second millennium B.C., the spring-watered hills of Israel saw the nomadic beginnings of the Israelite nation; through its desert wastes the Chosen People fled from their captivity in Egypt; and on its broad plains they fought a succession of invaders in defence of the Land promised by God. In its austere wilderness, Jesus fasted, and in its waters he baptized his followers.

Such is the heritage of modern Israel—a state that came into existence less than half a century ago, yet a place where every landscape holds echoes of an ancient past.

The Lord said to Abram, "Leave your native land, your relatives and your father's home, and go to a country that I am going to show you.

I will bless you and make your name famous, so that you will be a blessing."

Abram was a very rich man, with sheep, goats and cattle as well as silver and gold.

Genesis 12:1, 2; 13:2

The salt-clogged waters of the Dead Sea conceal the probable site of Sodom and Gomorrah, destroyed by God for their immorality.

Overlooking the Dead Sea is a pillar-like salt formation, one of several known as "Lot's wife".

Suddenly the Lord rained burning sulphur
on the cities of Sodom and Gomorrah,
and destroyed them and the whole valley,
along with all the people there
and everything that grew on the land.

But Lot's wife looked back
and was turned into a pillar of salt.

Genesis 19: 24-26

Then the Lord said to Moses,
"This is the land that I promised
Abram, Isaac and Jacob
I would give to their descendants.
I have let you see it,
but I will not let you go there."

Deuteronomy 34:4

In the Judaean desert, south of Jericho, a 13th-century mosque and a Muslim cemetery mark the site where—says Islamic legend—Moses lies buried.

Not long afterwards
Jesus came from Nazareth
and was baptized by John
in the Jordan.

As soon as Jesus came up
out of the water,
He saw heaven opening
and the Spirit coming down
on Him like a dove.

Mark 1: 9-10

The River Jordan, green-fringed in the fertile north of Israel, flows for 360 kilometres before disappearing into the Dead Sea.

Only a few kilometres from Jerusalem, the barren hills of the Judaean wilderness offered a retreat for those who, like John the Baptist and later Jesus

Then the Spirit led Jesus into the desert
to be tempted by the Devil.

After spending forty days and nights without food,
Jesus was hungry.

Then the Devil came to Him and said,
"If you are God's son,
order these stones to turn into bread."

Matthew 4: 1-3

himself, wished to devote themselves to fasting and meditation.

Two men fish the choppy waters of the Sea of Galilee, where Jesus found his first disciples—Simon (later called Peter), Andrew, James and John.

*As Jesus walked
along the shore of Lake Galilee,
He saw two fishermen,
Simon and his brother Andrew,
catching fish with a net.*

*Jesus said to them, "Come with me,
and I will teach you to catch men."*

Mark 1:16-17

From the gentle slope of the Mount of Olives—now dominated by the spires of a Russian Orthodox church—Jesus rode in triumph into Jerusalem.

*They came to a place called Gethsemane,
and Jesus said to his disciples,
"Sit here while I pray."*

*He went a little farther on,
threw Himself on the ground, and prayed.*

Mark 14:32, 35

Ancient olive trees cast their shade in the Garden of Gethsemane, where Jesus prayed before his arrest.

CENTURIES OF EXILE AND RETURN

Throughout their long, stateless centuries, the Jews never lost their yearning for the Promised Land. Three times a day during prayers the pious would repeat the words: "Sound the great horn for our freedom, lift up the banner to gather our exiles and gather us from the four corners of the earth to our land." They were not advocating a practical policy: the Return was scheduled for "the end of days" and would take place under the divine authority of the Messiah, come at last to deliver the Chosen People. The duty of the Jews, in the interminable meantime, was to keep the faith; in short, to remember.

No people, perhaps, has more to remember than the Jews. Their recorded history is longer than that of any other race. The exile that began almost 2,000 years ago and ended with the birth of modern Israel in 1948 is merely one episode in their saga.

In the second millennium B.C., the Patriarch Abraham, spurred by the heavenly command to found a nation of people who would serve a single deity, set off with his flocks and his kin from the ancient city of Ur, near the Persian Gulf, to the land of Canaan, lying roughly between the River Jordan, the Dead Sea and the Mediterranean. "Unto thy seed," said the One God to Abraham, in Genesis, "will I give this land." Such was the promise that inspired Abraham's heirs, the Israelites.

Here history blends inextricably with legend: Abraham may not have existed and the biblical account, which was written well after the supposed journey to Canaan, is more spiritual than historical. Nevertheless, archaeological evidence does not contradict it. Abraham, or a number of Abrahams, probably did make such a journey. The important part of the legend is that before the Jews were a people they were an idea; the monotheism of Abraham was a long way from fully developed Judaism, but it was even more distant from the fantastic polytheistic cults of the Patriarch's neighbours.

The next great step was the first exile. Driven by famine from Canaan, the Israelites moved to Egypt, where their status gradually changed from that of welcomed immigrants to a persecuted and enslaved minority. Around 1200 B.C., under the leadership of Moses (again possibly a legendary figure, though the archaeological record supports the outline of the story), they fled from their oppressors and journeyed across the Sinai peninsula until they came to Mount Sinai. At the summit, God gave Moses the Ten Commandments, which were to serve as the basis of both Judaic law (the Torah) and Christianity. Moses also received a renewed injunction to lead his people back to Canaan and there to create "a holy nation".

Henceforth, the story of the Jews moves steadily out of legend and into history. For two centuries, their nation developed without a central authority;

On a rock above the Dead Sea, the fortress of Masada stands as a potent symbol of the struggle against tyranny. It was here, in 73 A.D., that 960 Jewish resistance fighters—men, women and children—chose to commit mass suicide rather than yield to the besieging Romans.

2

In a medieval Haggadah—the ritual text for the feast of Passover—the Egyptian Pharaoh consults his wise men while a blue-robed Moses leads the escaping Israelites through the Red Sea. The annual Passover festival commemorates their flight from slavery in Egypt.

in the Bible this was the time of the Judges—divinely inspired individuals who were sometimes military heroes and sometimes judicial officials. The people were mostly small farmers, owing allegiance more to one of the 12 tribes into which they were divided than to the community as a whole.

But the threat from warlike neighbours, especially the Philistines, brought the 12 tribes together under a joint monarchy, and Israel entered the age of Kings: Saul, David and Solomon being the earliest. Their capital was Jerusalem; there, in the 10th century B.C., Solomon built the First Temple to house the Tablets of the Law that Moses had received on Sinai.

After Solomon's death, the old tribal feuds flared up again, and the nation split into two kingdoms—Israel, with its new capital of Samaria, in the north, and Judah, centred on Jerusalem, in the south. The division proved disastrous in the face of the rising empire of Assyria. In 721 B.C., the Assyrians descended from the north-east upon Samaria, laid it waste and carried off thousands of Israelites—the fabled "10 Lost Tribes"—into slavery.

Judah fared better. Although it was forced to accept Assyrian suzerainty, it continued to enjoy almost complete autonomy. Nevertheless, the country remained an easy prey for predatory powers. Over the next six centuries it was ruled, in turn, by Babylonians, Persians and Greeks.

The Jews retained a fierce national pride, however, and in 114 B.C., after almost 50 years of guerrilla warfare against their Greek masters, they finally succeeded in re-establishing an independent Judah.

Independence did not last for long. In 63 B.C., the country was overrun by

An illumination from a Jewish prayer book printed in 1470 depicts Haman, would-be slayer of the Persian Jews, executed with his 10 sons. Foiled by the King's Jewish wife, Haman was hanged and the Jews saved—an event marked by the festival of Purim.

yet another set of conquerors—the Romans. At first, they did little more than change the name of their new domain from Judah to Judaea. But gradually over the years, their rule became more oppressive. In 66 A.D., led by a group of militant patriots known as the Zealots, the Jewish population rose in open revolt. The Roman garrison of Jerusalem was massacred and a Roman army which was sent to retrieve the situation was cut to pieces.

For a while, the Jewish rebels were helped by a bitter civil war that had broken out within the Empire. But in 70 A.D., a powerful Roman army captured Jerusalem and the city was razed to the ground.

Jerusalem's fall marked the end of the so-called Great Revolt. The surviving Zealots fled to the fortress of Masada, on a grim, granite rock above the Dead Sea. Here they held out for another three years; even at the end, in the face of overwhelming odds, they refused to surrender. Instead, the Zealots killed first their wives and children, then themselves.

The spirit of resistance did not die at Masada. Less than 60 years later, Simon Bar-Kochba—"the son of a star"—led a new uprising that drove the Romans out of the country. They soon returned, however, and by 135 A.D. Jewish independence had been utterly crushed. It would not be seen again for another 1,813 years.

The damage done by the Great Revolt had been bad enough; the consequences of the Bar-Kochba rebellion were far worse. Whatever Jewish buildings had survived in Jerusalem were demolished and ploughed over, and by imperial decree all Jews were barred, on pain of death, from coming within sight of their ancient city, which was to be reconstructed as a Roman colony and renamed Aeolia Capitolina. The country itself was a waste, with many of its inhabitants dead or sold off as slaves. Even the name Judaea was obliterated from the maps. The land was to be called Syria Palaestina, after the most detested of the Jews' ancient enemies, the Philistines.

When the danger to Roman rule had passed, however, the Empire was satisfied, and it was not long before the synagogues and rabbinical academies of Palestine were flourishing once more. But the Jewish population had been decimated by war. Palestine remained the spiritual centre of the Jewish world, but its political and economic centre lay outside the homeland, among the Jews of the Diaspora.

The Diaspora, or Dispersal, was no new phenomenon. Jews had been leaving the homeland for centuries, and deportation by conquering armies was only one of the causes. Venturesome Jews had long sought their fortunes abroad and their communities were scattered throughout the Empire.

The oldest part of the Diaspora, in fact, was outside the Empire altogether, in Mesopotamia, once the homeland of Babylonians. In 586 B.C., the Babylonians had destroyed Jerusalem and led its people off into captivity, and a Babylonian Jewish community had existed ever since. The Babylonian Jews produced, by the end of the fifth century, one of the greatest of all Jewish achievements—the Talmud, or Teaching, a judicial, theological and practical guide that even today orders every aspect of observant Jewish life.

By the time the Talmud was completed, the situation of the Jews within the Roman Empire had deteriorated

2

sharply. The catalyst for their misfortunes was an edict proclaimed by the Emperor Constantine in 313 A.D., which made Christianity effectively the state religion. To evangelistic Christians, the Jews were anathema. Not only did they bear a blood-guilt for the crucifixion of Christ, but they persisted in denying Christ's divinity, claiming that the true Messiah had yet to appear. It followed, therefore, that they were not merely misguided, but were an unclean and pernicious sect deserving any form of persecution that Christians saw fit to inflict on them.

Within a few years of Constantine's edict, a mass of discriminatory laws were passed, stripping Jews of land and civil rights, and forcing them out of the mainstream of the economy. Soon synagogue-burning became a popular sport, and at the beginning of the fifth century, in Alexandria, Jews suffered their first full-scale massacre.

In Palestine itself, which the Roman Empire now regarded as not merely a province but as the Holy Land, the Jews were a small and persecuted minority, scraping a living in the most desolate corners of the country and entirely at the mercy of the assortment of bigoted monks, fanatical Christian pilgrims and simple Christian brigands who now largely inhabited it.

The other great world-conquering religion of the first millennium was kinder to the Jews. The new monotheistic creed of Islam arose in Arabia in the seventh century. The faith spread with extraordinary speed and by the eighth century its followers had created a vast Islamic Empire that stretched all the way from the borders of India to the Atlantic Ocean. Palestine itself was conquered in 638 A.D.

The Empire's Arab rulers, who

Holding a whip to symbolize his authority, the first-century Jewish sage, Rabban Gamaliel the Elder, addresses students. According to St. Paul's account in the New Testament, it was "at the feet of Gamaliel" that he received his own religious tuition.

wanted to make the most of the loyal service that Jews were willing to offer, not only allowed them to practise their religion without interference, but also freed them from the economic and cultural restrictions which had been imposed on them under Christianity. As a result, Jews reached high positions in every sphere of life, from trade to diplomacy. In Palestine, Jews were permitted to settle once more in Jerusalem, while returning exiles were given the right to claim back their land.

Islam reached Spain in 711 A.D., creating a hospitable environment for Jews already settled there. For many centuries thereafter, a rich Hispano–Judaic culture flourished. The Hebrew word for Spain was Sepharad, from which the Spanish Jews took the name of Sephardim. Intellectual life blossomed; Jewish scholarship made the University of Cordoba the greatest centre of learning in Europe.

The lessons of coexistence offered by the Islamic lands were not lost on the more perceptive rulers of the Christian West, who saw the advantages that their own Jewish communities could bring them. Not the least of these was the access to the web of trade and communications that Jews had painfully built up both in Christendom and in the Islamic world.

A period of relative calm and stability ensued for European Jewry. It was abruptly shattered in 1096, when France and other Western countries launched a Crusade to liberate Palestine from the Muslim infidels. Since the intention was to kill non-believers, many Christian warriors decided to start with the nearest Jews, so that the route to the Holy Land became littered with Jewish corpses.

And when, in 1099, the Crusaders

This sixth-century mosaic, discovered in a ruined Byzantine church at Medaba, near the Dead Sea, is the oldest known map of Jerusalem. More than 30 buildings can be identified on it, including the Damascus Gate *(below, left)* and the Church of the Holy Sepulchre *(below, centre)*.

eventually conquered Jerusalem, they marked their victory by the murder of every non-Christian in the city. The last surviving Jews were herded into a synagogue and burnt alive.

By the time the Muslims recaptured the Holy Land in 1291, anti-Semitism was endemic throughout Western Europe. Jews found themselves subjected to harsh taxation, sometimes forced to wear distinguishing badges, and penned into ghettoes—the word was first applied to the Jewish quarter of Venice in 1516, but the reality had long anticipated it.

Far from extinguishing the Jewish sense of identity, persecution strengthened it. Physical segregation, imposed by European authorities to prevent the contamination of Christians by Jews, was often welcomed by Jewish leaders as a means of preventing the reverse. Judaism depended on the observation of the Law; separation from Christians ensured that the Jews had no other law to seduce them.

After discrimination and persecution, there came massacres and mass expulsions: from England in 1290, from France in 1394, and finally, after the Christian reconquest, from the Sephardic heartland of Spain in 1492.

After the expulsions, the dividing lines of the Diaspora were even more diverse. The Sephardim travelled north, south and east, joining existing Jewish communities in Holland, North Africa and the Balkans. The German

55

Jews—the name Ashkenazim comes from the Hebrew word for the Germanic lands—moved mainly eastwards, into Poland, Lithuania and Russia. The two waves met in the territories of the Islamic Ottoman Empire, ruled by the sultans of Turkey, who offered not only a refuge but also a welcome.

In 1517, the Ottomans made themselves masters of Palestine, the homeland to which the Jews still looked back longingly in their prayers and traditions. It was to remain part of the Ottoman Empire for the next four centuries.

Not surprisingly, some of the more pious Jews took the opportunity of returning to Palestine. They went back, though, not as colonists but as pilgrims. According to their belief, the rebirth of the Jewish nation was something that could only be accomplished with the coming of the Messiah and the ingathering of his scattered people.

It was not, indeed, until the end of the 19th century that Jews began seriously to consider the idea of a Jewish nation created ahead of the Messiah's coming. The spur was the desperation of the Jews in tsarist Russia. Unlike their brethren in the West, who now enjoyed the fruits of emancipation, the Russian Jews continued to live under conditions hardly different from those their forebears had known in the Middle Ages. Denied all rights of citizenship, they were the helpless victims of both state oppression and mob violence.

Even so, the anti-Jewish frenzy that followed the assassination of Tsar Alexander II in 1881—as with all great calamities then, the Jews were held responsible—took the world by surprise. On a scale that had not been seen for more than a century, murder and arson ravaged the Jewish community and sent hundreds of thousands of terrified refugees streaming across Russia's frontiers. A new word entered the European vocabulary: pogrom.

The mass violence did more than drive Russian Jews westwards. It inspired in some of them a desperate conviction that freedom and safety were to be found only within the borders of a Jewish homeland. As Leo Pinsker, a Russian-Jewish physician, wrote in his book *Auto-Emancipation*, published in 1882, "We must re-establish ourselves as a living nation."

Some of Pinsker's young admirers tried to put this idea into practice, forming a back-to-Zion agricultural movement that they called BILU, from the Hebrew initials of the biblical phrase, "House of Jacob, come let us go!" But Palestine was far; money was scarce; and friends were few. The first party to make the return comprised precisely 16 people.

It was a very small beginning. It might have been the ending, too, but for the inspiration and energy of one man. Born in Budapest in 1860, Theodor Herzl was a journalist by trade. He was also at one time so indifferent a Jew that he felt that the mass baptism of Jewish children might be the answer to anti-Semitism.

His moment of truth came in 1894 when he went to Paris to cover the infamous Dreyfus trial. Captain Alfred Dreyfus, a Jewish officer in the French Army, was accused of being a German spy. The evidence of treason was slim, that of anti-Jewish prejudice strong; but what shocked the young Herzl was the crowd outside the courtroom, in supposedly enlightened France, baying "Death to the Jews!"

With the single-minded devotion of an Old Testament prophet, Herzl wrote one of the most influential tracts of all time: *The Jewish State*. He had heard of neither Pinsker nor the BILU movement. He was equally ignorant of the obstacles in his path, from the physical difficulties of colonizing Palestine to the opposition facing him from his fellow-Jews, especially the wealthiest and most influential.

Perhaps it was his ignorance that gave him strength, for by 1897 he was able to convene the first Zionist Congress, held in Basle, in Switzerland. Many Western Jews were horrified, believing that it would only encourage anti-Semitism and undermine the process of Jewish assimilation. Others, however, were less timid and the Congress turned out to be a triumphant success. Afterwards, Herzl declared, "At Basle, I created the Jewish State. In five years, perhaps, and certainly in fifty, everyone will see it." It was the sort of outrageous statement only a visionary can make. Incredibly, it turned out to be true.

Over the next few years, Herzl was tireless, knocking at every possible door, seeking help from the governments of France, Britain and Germany, negotiating with the Sultan of Turkey, even pleading with the Pope. Yet still the great prize remained out of reach, and Herzl, exhausted by his efforts, died in 1904, aged 44.

The Zionist movement had little

A contemporary painting shows the 16th-century Turkish sultan, Suleiman the Magnificent, receiving a foreign ambassador. Although the Holy Land prospered under Suleiman's rule, decline set in with his death, and for the next three and a half centuries Palestine languished.

time to mourn him: there was much to do, not least in Palestine itself. Like the rest of the Ottoman Empire, the country had fallen into chronic decay, with the result that it was now largely barren, exploited by corrupt Turkish officials and ravaged by drought, banditry and disease. The Zionist pioneers remained undaunted, however, and by 1914 they had managed to set up 44 settlements, an agricultural school and a technical college.

Over this scene of gradual progress World War I burst like a thunderclap. With the great powers locked in conflict, it seemed unlikely that any of them would be paying much attention to the Zionists. Worse still, Turkey and Russia were on different sides—the former had lined up with Germany and Austria, and the latter with France and Britain. This meant that the majority of Palestine Jews, being of Russian origin, were regarded by the Turks as enemy aliens, and many were expelled from the country. It was this period of cataclysmic upheaval, however, that was to bring Zionism its greatest triumph so far.

One of the leading Zionists, Dr. Chaim Weizmann (by origin a Russian Jew), was a chemist of world stature lecturing at Manchester University. A discovery he had made in explosives manufacture brought him into contact with the highest levels of the British government, and he used every opportunity to advance his people's claim.

By the winter of 1916, the British were prepared to do more than just listen. The war was going badly: Britain was blockaded by German U-boats; Russia was on the brink of revolution and collapse; and the United States was still hesitating to enter the conflict. But if the American and Russian Jews

A CHRONOLOGY OF KEY EVENTS

c.7000 B.C. Neolithic settlers build Jericho, the oldest known city, complete with wall, temple and moat.

c.2000 B.C. Abraham, the biblical patriarch from whom Jewish people trace their ancestry, travels from Mesopotamia to the Land of Canaan.

c.1700–1290 B.C. Driven by famine from Canaan into Egypt, the Israelites are gradually reduced to slavery.

c.1290 B.C. Moses leads the Israelites out of Egypt. During their 40 years of wandering in the deserts of Sinai they receive the Ten Commandments.

c.1250–1225 B.C. Joshua leads the 12 tribes of Israel back into the Promised Land of Canaan.

c.1020 B.C. Under Saul, the Israelites establish a monarchy in an effort to resist expansion of the Philistines.

c.1004 B.C. Saul falls in battle against the Philistines and the kingdom is split between the northern and southern groups of tribes.

c.998–965 B.C. The kingdom reunites under David, who crushes the Philistines and makes Jerusalem his capital.

c.965–926 B.C. The crown passes to David's son, Solomon, *(above)*, who erects the First Temple in Jerusalem.

c.926 B.C. With Solomon's death, the country splits once more. The northern kingdom calls itself Israel and the southern kingdom becomes Judah.

733 B.C. Judah submits to the growing might of the Assyrians.

721 B.C. Israel is conquered by the Assyrians and many of its people—the "Ten Lost Tribes"—are deported.

598–586 B.C. Nebuchadnezzar, king of the Babylonians, rules Judah as a vassal state. Twelve years later, following a Jewish revolt, Nebuchadnezzar destroys Jerusalem, including the Temple, and deports most of the population to Babylon.

538 B.C. Cyrus, king of the Persians, conquers Babylon and grants Jews permission to return to Jerusalem and rebuild the Temple.

332 B.C. Alexander the Great brings Judah under Macedonian rule.

198 B.C. Judah is conquered by the Seleucid rulers of Syria.

167–114 B.C. A Jewish revolt against the Seleucids is crushed and the warrior-patriot, Judah Maccabee, dies in battle. But a prolonged guerrilla war ends with the re-establishment of Jewish independence.

63 B.C. Judah is occupied by the Romans, who rename it Judaea.

33 A.D. Jesus is crucified at Golgotha *(below)*.

66–74 The Jews, inspired by a militant group known as the Zealots, launch the Great Revolt against Rome. The Romans destroy Jerusalem, including the Second Temple, and the surviving Zealots take refuge at the fortress of Masada. Outnumbered by Romans, they prefer suicide to capture.

132–135 Final revolt of the Jews against Rome is led by Simon Bar-Kochba. After three years, the revolt is crushed. Jews are prohibited from entering Jerusalem and Judaea is renamed Syria Palaestina as a reminder of their ancient foes, the Philistines.

325 Constantine I, the first Christian Emperor, begins the transformation of Jerusalem into a Christian city.

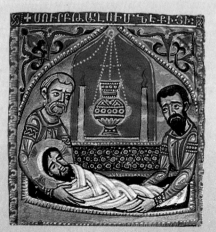

638 Palestine is conquered by the Arabs. For the next 460 years, the country remains under Muslim rule.

691 Caliph Abd al-Malik completes the building of the Dome of the Rock, one of Islam's holiest shrines.

1096 Prompted by an appeal from Pope Urban II, soldiers of France and other Christian lands launch a Crusade to free Palestine from Muslim rule.

1099–1291 Having conquered Jerusalem, the Crusaders try to turn Palestine into a Christian kingdom. But their rule is threatened by continual rebellion and invasion. In 1187, Jerusalem itself is captured by the Kurdish leader, Saladin, and 104 years later, the last Crusader stronghold of Acre falls to the Mameluke Turks, now undisputed masters of the Holy Land.

1517 The Mamelukes are defeated by the Turkish sultan Selim I. For the next four centuries Palestine remains a province of the Ottoman Empire.

1882 Large-scale violence against Russian Jews prompts the publication of Leo Pinsker's *Auto-Emancipation*, urging the creation of a Jewish national home. Several thousand Jews from Europe travel to Palestine to set up agricultural communities *(above)*.

1896–1897 Theodor Herzl publishes *The Jewish State*, calling for the creation of a Jewish state by international agreement. Herzl organizes the first Zionist Congress at Basle, Switzerland.

1914–1918 In World War I, the Ottoman Empire sides with Germany and Austria against France, Britain and Russia.

1917 British Foreign Secretary Balfour declares his government favours "the establishment in Palestine of a National Home for the Jewish people". Weeks later, British troops enter Jerusalem.

1920 The League of Nations assigns Britain a mandate to govern Palestine. Jewish immigration is renewed.

1933 The Nazi takeover in Germany leads to a massive increase in Jewish immigration to Palestine.

1936–1939 A campaign of violence by the Palestine Arabs results in almost 5,000 casualties, including 2,849 killed.

1939–1945 During World War II, most Palestine Jews support the British war effort. But British restrictions on Jewish immigration eventually provoke a campaign of bombing and shooting by Jewish extremist groups.

1947 Britain refers the Palestine problem to the United Nations, which votes to partition the country into Arab and Jewish states. The plan is rejected by the Arabs, who renew their attacks on the Jewish population.

1948 The British withdraw and the State of Israel is proclaimed. A day later, the new state is invaded by the armies of five Arab countries.

1949 Israel signs armistice agreements with its Arab neighbours. Jordan bars Israeli access to holy sites in East Jerusalem. Chaim Weizmann is elected Israel's first President, with David Ben-

Gurion as Prime Minister.

1950 The Knesset—Israel's parliament—passes the Law of Return, confirming the right of every Jew to live in Israel.

1956 Egypt nationalizes the Suez Canal, provoking military action by France and Britain. Israel attacks Egyptian bases in Sinai and succeeds in opening the Gulf of Aqaba (Eilat) to Israeli ships.

1962 Twelve stained glass windows by artist Marc Chagall, depicting the 12 Tribes of Israel, are installed in the synagogue of the Hadassah Medical Centre, Jerusalem *(left)*.

1964 Arab leaders set up the Palestine Liberation Organization (PLO).

1967 In the Six Day War, Israel wrests the Golan Heights, Sinai, the Gaza Strip and East Jerusalem from the Arabs. The Knesset later approves annexation of the Golan Heights and East Jerusalem, declaring the reunited city "the capital of Israel for all time".

1968 The PLO steps up its terrorist campaign against Israel.

1969 Golda Meir is installed as Israel's fourth Prime Minister *(below)*.

1973 Egypt and Syria choose the Jewish Day of Atonement to launch an attack against Israeli positions on the Golan Heights and in Sinai, sparking off the Yom Kippur War. Israel retains the Golan Heights, but gives up land in

Sinai to Egypt. Israel's first Prime Minister, David Ben-Gurion, dies.

1977 Egyptian President Sadat meets Israeli leaders in Jerusalem *(below)*.

1979 Under the terms of a peace treaty signed with Egypt, Israel agrees to pull out its remaining forces in Sinai.

1982–1985 Israel's attempt to drive the PLO out of Lebanon leads to fighting between the Christians and their Druze, Muslim and Palestinian rivals. After the massacre of 800 Palestine civilians by members of a Christian militia force linked to Israel, Israeli Defence Minister, Ariel Sharon, resigns.

1986 Israel's annual inflation rate—having reached a high of almost 450 per cent in 1984—is reduced to about 22 per cent by such measures as a budget cut, devaluation of the shekel, and wage and price freezes.

2

could be persuaded to use their influence on behalf of the Allies, then the situation might be transformed.

Such, at any rate, was the view of the British government. On November 2, 1917, Foreign Secretary Arthur Balfour issued the declaration that forever afterwards bore his name.

The key paragraph read: "His Majesty's Government view with favour the establishment in Palestine of a national home for the Jewish people, and will use their best endeavours to facilitate the achievement of this object, it being clearly understood that nothing shall be done which may prejudice the civil and religious rights of existing non-Jewish communities in Palestine, or the rights and political status enjoyed by Jews in any other country."

It was worded with studied vagueness: it had to be. The British had also been making promises to the Arabs in the Ottoman Empire, with the object of encouraging them (successfully, as it turned out) to revolt against their masters. It was going to be difficult, after the war, to reconcile these pledges.

Nevertheless, the Balfour Declaration represented an astonishing commitment on the part of a great imperial power. And although it was intended primarily to advance British interests, many of those involved, including Balfour himself, acted out of a genuine sense of idealism. Certainly, it was a triumph for Weizmann's quiet, ceaseless diplomacy—the result, he said later, of 2,000 interviews. (Although he was not elected head of the World Zionist Organization until 1920, he had long been its leading advocate.)

Of course, it was only a beginning: the Balfour Declaration carefully avoided any mention of Jewish statehood. Weizmann himself warned his fellow-Zionists that "States must be built up slowly, gradually, systematically and patiently". But now, at least, there was something to build on.

Barely five weeks after the Balfour

Members of Hashomer—the first Jewish armed force in modern Palestine—pose with their commander Israel Shohat *(centre)*. Founded in the early 1900s to protect Jewish settlements, the force recruited only the best horsemen and the finest shots.

Declaration, British troops entered Jerusalem. In the following September, a second offensive brought the whole Ottoman Empire down in ruins. It capitulated in late October, a few days before the fall of Germany. Zionists everywhere looked forward optimistically to receiving their due reward.

So, also, did a great many other people. The British, for example, were determined to retain control of the entire area around the Suez Canal, which had become the British Empire's strategic obsession. The French also had imperial ambitions, centred on Syria and Lebanon. And the Arabs, freed at last from the Ottoman yoke, had powerful aspirations of their own.

Between the Arabs and the Zionists, at least, it had seemed that some sort of compromise might be possible. In the closing months of the war, a Zionist Commission, headed by Chaim Weizmann, had visited Palestine. Weizmann himself had met and negotiated with the Emir Feisal, the principal leader of the Arab Revolt. The Emir, wrote Weizmann, "was eager to see Jews and Arabs working in harmony", and for the rest of his life the great Zionist remained convinced that the bitter conflicts which followed in later years could have been avoided.

However, in 1920, the Allies decided on a Middle East settlement that left the Arabs both angry and embittered. France was assigned a League of Nations mandate to govern Syria, and at the same time Britain received the mandate for Palestine. The Balfour pledge was incorporated in the terms of the Palestine Mandate, and the world Zionist movement was recognized as the appropriate "Jewish Agency" for co-operating with and assisting the British in building the National Home.

In this 1850 lithograph, a party of Polish Jews waits to embark at Jaffa after a pilgrimage to Jerusalem. The 19th century brought many returning exiles to the city of David and Solomon, a focus of aspiration in the centuries of dispersion.

The high hopes of Arab independence were to a large extent crushed, and from then on the Arabs were in no mood for compromise with anyone.

The Zionists, though, were also in a difficult position. At the war's end, Jews accounted for barely 10 per cent of Palestine's 750,000 inhabitants. Only a small fraction of these Jews were Zionist sympathizers: most of them lived in pious communities devoted to Talmudic study, supported by Diaspora charity and utterly uninterested in anything so worldly as a Jewish state. To make the Zionist dream a reality, massive immigration was essential.

But the British, fearful of Arab reaction, were unwilling to permit it. Zionists had cheered when the British government named Sir Herbert (later Lord) Samuel—who was himself a Jew—as the first High Commissioner of Palestine. Samuel, however, was first and foremost a representative of the British Crown, who felt that his Jewishness obliged him to lean towards the Arabs. Shortly after his arrival, he granted the office of Grand Mufti of Jerusalem—and with it the religious leadership of Arab Palestine—to one Haj Amin El Husseini, a passionate young nationalist who had fled the country in 1920 to escape imprisonment for inciting anti-Jewish riots. In 1921, the new Mufti celebrated his appointment by stirring up fresh riots. To Zionist fury, Samuel responded not by arresting the Mufti, but by restricting Jewish immigration.

Samuel, in fact, was taking much the same view as Weizmann himself: that the National Home described in the Balfour Declaration would come about in years rather than months, and that any attempt to hurry the process could only lead to disaster. It was a view that events in Europe were soon to shatter.

The immediate problem—at least, for the Zionists—was not the ban on mass immigration, but the lack of pres-

אַיער אַלטנײלאַנד דאַרף אױך האָבען!

בּת - ציון

שליסט זיך אָן אין דעם אידישען רעגימענט.

sure for immigration of any kind. The Russian Jews, who had provided most of the early colonists, were now sealed inside the new Soviet Union, and the Jews who lived in Western Europe and the United States were increasingly reluctant to exchange the comfort and security they enjoyed there for a precarious existence in Palestine. By the late 1920s, the future of the National Home looked shaky indeed. In 1927, 2,000 more Jews abandoned the country than came to it; in 1928, the net surplus amounted to 10 people.

It was 1929 that proved to be the most critical year since the war. The Zionist Congress, at their meeting that August in Zürich, endorsed Weizmann's proposals for an extended Jewish Agency which would involve the whole of the Diaspora—both the Zionists and the non-Zionists—in the future of Palestine. The decision had more to do with fund-raising than power politics, but it aroused fears among the Palestine Arabs that they were at the mercy of just the sort of worldwide Jewish conspiracy that anti-Semites had been ranting about for decades.

Their fears were inflamed even further by Weizmann's hard-line critic, Vladimir Jabotinsky, who derided any policy which might be construed as appeasement of the Arabs. What Jabotinsky demanded, instead, was an influx of "great colonizing masses" that would establish a Jewish state "on either side of the Jordan". (Although originally part of Palestine, the land immediately to the east of the river had been incorporated into the Emirate of Trans-Jordan, later to become the Hashemite Kingdom of Jordan.) The result was the worst outbreak of violence so far in the Mandate's his-

tory. Before British troops could be summoned from Egypt, 133 Jews had died at the hands of Arabs, including 60 members of an ancient, and non-Zionist, religious community. The British authorities put down the rioting, which at times seemed closer to a rebellion, but afterwards attempted to apportion blame between the two communities. This naturally infuriated the Jews, who saw themselves, with some justification, as entirely innocent victims. The net effect was thus not only an increase in Arab-Jewish hostility, but a deep-rooted Jewish resentment of the British administration.

The British, in fact, had long held the view that the peaceful implementation of the Balfour Declaration was an impossibility. They reacted characteristically by sending a series of Royal Commissions to study the problem. It was less a policy than a means of marking time. Unfortunately, events unfolding in Europe meant that Britain would have no time to mark.

In January 1933, Adolf Hitler became Chancellor of Germany, inaugurating the most appalling persecution in all of Jewish history. The immediate re-

sult was a huge increase in immigration to Palestine; from 9,553 in 1932, the numbers leapt to the unprecedented level of 61,854 in 1935. The flood of refugees provoked the inevitable Arab response. By 1936, a full-scale rebellion had broken out.

The rising continued for six months, after which the British appointed yet another Royal Commission. The report of this Commission, published in 1937, recommended the end of the Mandate and the partition of Palestine into autonomous Jewish and Arab areas. The Jews were inclined to accept the scheme, but the British government considered the partition proposals to be unworkable (as, indeed, did the League of Nations itself).

This did not prevent the Arabs, however, from believing that they were to

Jews gather on a sandy wasteland near Jaffa in 1909 to parcel out building plots for the proposed suburb of Tel Aviv—Hill of Spring. Swelled by waves of immigration, Greater Tel Aviv is now the largest Israeli city, with a population of some 1,555,000.

become the victims of further Zionist machinations. In the summer of 1937, a second revolt erupted. This time the killing was to go on for two years. Nor were the Arabs of Palestine the only ones to express their outrage at Britain's supposed truckling to the Zionists. A Pan-Arab conference declared: "Britain must change her policy or we shall be at liberty to side with other European powers whose policies are inimical to Great Britain."

By now, the war clouds gathering over Europe were obvious even to the appeasement-minded government of Neville Chamberlain, and the threat did not fall upon deaf ears. In a war with Germany, the British knew that the Jews would have no alternative but to fight at their side; the Arabs, on the other hand, could easily create serious

difficulties, threatening military bases and oil supplies.

For the British government, therefore, the choice was clear. In May 1939 it published a White Paper—that is, a declaration of policy—on Palestine that shocked and infuriated Jewish opinion. A total of 25,000 Jewish immigrants would be allowed to enter the country immediately; but no more than 10,000 a year would be admitted over the next five years, and thereafter none at all, unless the Arabs agreed (which seemed hardly likely). After 10 years, there was to be established an independent Arab Palestine in which only 5 per cent of the land would be available for Jewish settlement.

What this White Paper amounted to was a virtual repudiation of the Balfour Declaration, and the Jews were under-

standably bitter. As David Ben-Gurion, the head of the Jewish Agency Executive, stated after the British declaration of war on Germany: "We shall fight with Great Britain in this war as if there were no White Paper, and we shall fight the White Paper as if there were no war."

More disappointment came when the British refused to allow the Zionists to raise a Jewish Army; some 30,000 Palestine Jews, nevertheless, enlisted as individuals in the British Forces. Quite apart from their contribution to the defeat of Nazi Germany, it was becoming clear to Zionist leaders that men with military training were likely to be a vital asset in the years to come.

They already had the *Haganah*—literally, "Defence"—a clandestine force that had existed in Palestine, with

2

the tacit connivance of the British authorities, since the early 1920s. During the troubled Thirties, the Haganah had provided Jewish settlements with their main protection against Arab attack; some of its members had even received training from the British. In effect, it was the military arm of the Jewish Agency, and at the outset of the Second World War it co-operated with the British to such an extent that it was more or less legally recognized.

As the war progressed, two other small, armed Jewish groups began to make their presence felt—and both were entirely illegal. The first was the *Irgun (Irgun Tsva'i Leumi*, or National Military Organization), extremists who had split from the Haganah. The second was the Freedom Fighters of Israel, better known as the Stern Group, itself an offshoot of the Irgun. Increasingly frustrated by British policy, they turned to outright terrorism.

The key issue, as always, was immigration. Ever since 1939, boatloads of desperate Jewish refugees had been reaching the shores of Palestine only to be turned away by British warships. The mandatory policy was to receive immigrants only up to the White Paper quota. Any immigrants above the quota were shipped off to detention camps either in Palestine itself or in some other part of the British Empire. By 1942, when the first inklings of the fate of Europe's Jews in the Nazi "Final Solution" reached the outside world, British policy began to seem to most Jews to be not merely anti-Zionist but downright murderous.

The growing tension was reflected in a near-split in the Zionist movement. Against the patient gradualism of Dr. Weizmann—who was still negotiating for a Jewish Army—there arose a younger, angrier faction motivated by a passionate sense of urgency and led by David Ben-Gurion. It had had enough of negotiating. Instead, Ben-Gurion demanded "that the gates of Palestine be opened . . . and that Palestine be established as a Jewish Commonwealth, integrated in the structure of the new democratic world."

The extremists of the Irgun and the Stern Group, ignoring opposition from Ben-Gurion and the other mainstream Zionist leaders, set about achieving the "Jewish Commonwealth" with the bullet and the bomb. In a public declaration issued in 1944, the Irgun announced that "There is no longer any armistice between the Jewish people and the British Administration which hands our brothers over to Hitler. Our people are at war with this regime, war to the end."

The surrender of Nazi Germany— and, soon afterwards, the election in Britain of an avowedly pro-Zionist Labour government—brought only the briefest of respites. In peacetime as well as in war, no British government was willing to accept the wholesale alienation of the Arab world that would result from the entry into Palestine of large numbers of Jewish refugees.

While British ministers, led by Foreign Secretary Ernest Bevin, engaged in a series of fruitless negotiations with Jewish and Arab delegations in London, the situation in Palestine went from bad to worse. Even the Haganah, for so long an example of moderation and restraint, carried out a large number of sabotage attacks that left the country's communications in chaos.

At this juncture, the United States President, Harry S. Truman, infuriated the British leaders by supporting a Jewish Agency demand that 100,000 Jewish refugees be allowed immediate entry to Palestine. However, the British Prime Minister, Clement Attlee, had good reasons for avoiding an open breach with the Americans. In addition to trying to secure a vital dollar loan for his war-exhausted country, he was also hoping to persuade the Americans to take over some of Britain's responsibilities in Palestine.

Truman proved amenable on the first point, but would not be moved on the second, and the most that Attlee was able to achieve was the appointment of an Anglo-American Committee of Inquiry "to examine political, economic and social conditions in Palestine as they bear upon the problem of Jewish immigration". The Committee published its report in April 1946: the 100,000 immigrants should be admitted—but into a bi-national state under British protection, where Jew and Arab lived in harmony.

Unfortunately, no such state existed, or was ever likely to exist. Even if it had been a possibility, the British would have had little enthusiasm for protecting it. Too many British servicemen had already died at the hands of the terrorists and the level of violence was steadily rising. In June, the Haganah destroyed the Allenby bridge across the Jordan and blew up 13 aircraft at Lydda airport (though both operations were conducted without loss of life).

This time, the Palestine Administration decided to hit back hard by ordering the arrest not only of the Haganah commanders, but of the Jewish Agency leaders as well. A few weeks later, the Irgun carried out its own retaliation by blowing up a wing of the King David Hotel, in Jerusalem, part of which was used as British Army Headquarters. British, Jews and Arabs were among

After World War II, British troops board the *Exodus 1947*, an immigrant ship rammed by the Royal Navy and towed into Haifa. Anxious to avoid provoking the Arabs, the ruling British had imposed severe curbs on Jewish entry to Palestine, but many ships tried to land their cargoes illegally.

the 91 dead and 45 injured.

In his fury, the commanding officer in Palestine issued an order forbidding his men to fraternize with the Jews, which would "punish them in a way the race dislikes—through their pockets". Worse still, some of the British troops were starting to take the law into their own hands. A grisly series of atrocities and counter-atrocities began.

Politically, the situation remained equally grim. It was not helped by a belligerent Bevin, who declared at the Labour Party Conference of June 1946 that the reason the Americans were pressing for the admission of Jewish refugees to Palestine was "because they don't want them in New York". Given the American controls on immigration then in force, there was enough truth in the gibe to hurt, and the Americans never forgave him.

Anglo-American relations were still further strained when President Truman declared himself in favour of a partition scheme proposed, from Paris, by David Ben-Gurion and other Jewish Agency leaders who had escaped the British round-up. Exasperated, Bevin explained his reason for rejecting the plan: "The Arabs won't accept partition. Am I to force it on them with British bayonets?"

Even now, Bevin was still hoping for a negotiated settlement. As a goodwill gesture, the imprisoned Jewish Agency leaders were released and a batch of illegal immigrants who had been detained in Cyprus were admitted to Palestine. Something of the same spirit of conciliation appeared at the Zionist Congress of December 1946. Dr Weizmann made a powerful speech warning delegates of the dangers of violence: "If you think of bringing the redemption nearer by un-Jewish methods, if you

2

lose faith in hard work and better days, then you commit idolatry and endanger what we have built . . . 'Zion shall be redeemed in Judgement'—and not by any other means.''

But it was too late. There was no conceivable proposal the British could make that would gain even grudging acceptance from both the Jews and the Arabs. And Dr. Weizmann, although revered as the Grand Old Man of Zionism, had long since passed the mantle of real leadership to others, notably Ben-Gurion, who were determined that "redemption" would be brought about by whatever means were necessary.

Finally, in February 1947, the des-

pairing British referred the whole of the problem to the United Nations. A U.N. Special Commission on Palestine (UNSCOP) was set up. In a majority report, published on September 1, it recommended the partition of the country into a small Jewish state, a larger Arab state and an internationally administered Jerusalem. The Jews accepted the report. The Arabs and the British did not.

The British had had enough. In addition to being the targets of a ruthless terrorist campaign, they were also incurring worldwide odium for their treatment of those who had survived the Nazi Holocaust. Now, even "in the

absence of a settlement", as the Colonial Secretary put it, Britain "had to plan for an early withdrawal of British forces and of the British Administration from Palestine."

In November, the UNSCOP proposals were accepted by the United Nations General Assembly in a modified form that meant more territory for the Arabs. The Americans and the Russians, in a rare display of unanimity, both voted in favour. Even in its new form, the plan was again accepted by the Jews and again rejected by the Arabs and the British.

However, the future of Palestine was no longer in the hands of the diplo-

mats—if, indeed, it ever had been. When news of the Assembly's decision reached the Palestinian Arabs, they immediately went on the rampage, killing, burning and looting from one end of the country to the other. The Haganah, which the British had systematically been trying to suppress for months, took time to mobilize. Meanwhile, Jewish casualties mounted. The British, to their discredit, did little to stop the violence. In many instances, troops and police stood idly by while the rioters did their work; more than once, the guardians of law and order openly expressed their approval.

Even at an official level, there was little attempt made at neutrality. The Haganah, desperately short of weapons, was subject to constant harrassment and arms searches. Illegal Jewish immigrants—and potential Haganah recruits—were turned away by the Royal Navy while armed Arab bands entered the country unmolested from Syria. As one British officer wrote later, "With the machinery of the Palestine Government still in position, with officials still going to their offices every morning, with the police in the streets and a considerable army still in its barracks, raging battles were going on in the country unhindered." In December, amidst the chaos, the British announced that they would terminate the Mandate on May 15, 1948.

For the Jews, the early months of the struggle were the most critical. The Haganah clung desperately to every scrap of Jewish territory, expending its greatest effort in sending supply convoys through Arab ambushes to outlying settlements and, above all, to the isolated Jewish community in Jerusalem. The greatest problem was lack of arms, and the Chief of Britain's Imper-

ial General Staff, Field Marshal Sir Bernard (later Lord) Montgomery, was not alone in believing that the Jews had "bought it". But an arms shipment purchased from Czechoslovakia—with Russian approval—arrived in March and turned the balance.

However, the Jews now found themselves threatened from a completely unexpected quarter. In the United States, Dr. Weizmann had worked tirelessly to win the support of President Truman and he seemed to have succeeded. But the American oil lobby, with its increasing interests in the Middle East, had been applying powerful pressure on the State Department to adopt a pro-Arab policy. In the same fateful month of March, the Americans suddenly switched course.

The American Ambassador to the United Nations called for a suspension of the partition scheme and suggested a temporary United Nations trusteeship over Palestine, "without prejudice to the character of the eventual political settlement". Weizmann addressed a last plea to the White House: "The choice before us, Mr. President, is between statehood and extermination." President Truman, embarrassed by the U.S. turnabout, gave Weizmann a promise. If a Jewish state were proclaimed, he told him, he would recognize it immediately.

There was little time to waste. The fighting in Palestine was becoming steadily more bitter. It was a war of populations, not just of soldiers, and the front line ran through every town and village. By the last week of April, 300,000 Arabs had left the country. But beyond its frontiers, the armies of five Arab nations were only waiting for the British to quit before they invaded.

At 9 a.m. on May 14, the last British High Commissioner left Palestine. A day ahead of schedule, the Mandate was over. At 4 p.m. on the same day, David Ben-Gurion read Israel's proclamation of independence to Jewish leaders gathered in the Tel Aviv Museum of Modern Art. (Various names had been suggested for the new state, including Judaea, Zion and *Eretz Israel*—Land of Israel. The vote had been in favour of Ben-Gurion's suggestion, Israel.) Truman kept his word. He immediately gave the new state provisional but effective recognition; and the Soviet Union followed within hours with full *de jure* recognition.

After almost 2,000 years, the Jews had finally reclaimed the Promised Land. The problem now was whether they would be able to defend it.

With his bicycle—a favourite mode of
kibbutz transportation—propped
nearby, an elderly resident mans the
gate of the collective. Every kibbutz has
its small guardhouse, today less a
security measure than a symbol of the
community's traditional watchfulness.

THE SELF-CONTAINED WORLD OF THE KIBBUTZ

Each week, in a small settlement on Israel's Mediterranean coast, 500 men and women crowd into their communal dining hall to vote on issues ranging from their children's education to family clothing budgets. They are kibbutzniks, members of one of several hundred agricultural and industrial collectives scattered throughout the country from the Golan Heights in the north to the southern reaches of the Negev. Whether they pick avocados in the kibbutz's orchards, manage its plastics factory or change nappies in its nursery, all kibbutzniks share equally in the ownership of the commune, which provides for their material and social needs from infancy to old age.

With only 3.5 per cent of the population living this communal life, the kibbutz movement's contributions to Israeli society far surpass its size. As well as producing nearly half of the nation's agricultural exports, the kibbutzim turn out a high proportion of its political and military leaders: in the Six Day War, for example, nearly one quarter of all army officers were kibbutzniks.

The kibbutz's newest housing, white concrete buildings each divided into four flats, provides families with balcony views across a grassy meadow. Homes are allocated according to seniority and size of family.

RESIDENTS AND WORKING GUESTS

The afternoon sun warms kibbutz volunteers, as well as drying their towels. Young people from around the world work on the collective for periods from one month to one year, performing unskilled jobs in return for room and board, some pocket money and a taste of communal living.

Students in the collective's intensive Hebrew course are given a lesson on the grass after devoting half their day to labour with the kibbutzniks. Many collectives have residential language programmes, permitting new immigrants and tourists—Jews and non-Jews—to learn Hebrew together.

After a day's work that began at dawn, a husband and wife find time to read and play with their young children. Families decorate their modest but comfortable flats according to their own tastes, although their budget for furnishings is determined by an allowance from the community.

A cafeteria-style meal brings
kibbutzniks and their visitors together
in the communal dining hall, the
collective's largest building. Their flats
are equipped with small kitchens, but
members prefer the lively bustle of the
hall for most meals.

A cluster of brightly dressed toddlers
waits for the trained kibbutznik nurse
to ferry them round the commune in
their infant cart. This kibbutz—unlike
some—allows children to sleep in their
parents' home, but youngsters spend
their days together from infancy
through 12 years of schooling.

Below a notice board displaying
information and messages for
residents, a woman checks the roster of
weekly job assignments. While the
kibbutz movement supports equality of
the sexes, women still predominate in
the traditional female domains of the
kitchen and nursery.

SHARED EFFORTS FOR SHARED WEALTH

In one of the kibbutz's 50 man-made ponds, freshwater fish gathered in nets are sucked out through a yellow vacuum tube for sorting and packing. Because many of its first members were fishermen by trade, this commune took up fish farming to provide them with work close to home.

Men of the kibbutz tend a banana grove, where blue plastic wrappings protect the fruit from frosts and birds. Begun primarily as agricultural collectives, kibbutzim today have diversified economies: some 80 per cent of this particular collective's wealth comes from its plastics factory.

A group of pious Jews, their heads
covered in accordance with ancient
custom, worship behind prayer tables
at Jerusalem's Western Wall. The
48 metre wall, last remnant of the
Temple destroyed by the Romans in
70 A.D., is cherished as a potent
symbol of national survival.

THE MAKING OF AN ISRAELI

It is early evening in Israel. In Tel Aviv's Mann Auditorium, viola player Rachel Kam and her fellow members of the Israel Philharmonic Orchestra wait for the conductor to lead them into a Mozart symphony. Down at the northern edge of the Negev, in the town of Sederot, factory worker Yonathan Angel, his Polish wife Eliana and their three sons have finished the evening meal and are listening to Gershwin's *Porgy and Bess* on their French-made stereo. His Sederot neighbours and co-workers—Iraqis, Tunisians, Kurds and Eastern Europeans—are studying their coupons for the state-run Sportoto lottery, working out the best odds for winning a spectacular cash prize.

In a courtyard in Jerusalem several pale young men in the velour hats and long black coats of an 18th-century Polish ghetto dispute a point of scripture. Up the coast, in a Haifa cake-shop, a table of elderly Germans consume *Apfelstrudel* and argue about Marx and Freud. Meanwhile, on a kibbutz in the Galilee, the 18-year-old daughter of Canadian immigrants is packing her case for her first stint of army service.

At first glance there seems nothing unusual about this mosaic of lifestyles and origins. Many Western nations have populations almost as varied. But the very ordinariness of the scene is itself extraordinary. It is evidence that for the first time in 2,000 years, Jews—history's perennial outcasts and wanderers—are at last free to live together in a homeland of their own.

Just over one quarter of the world's Jewish population now resides in Israel. The 3.5 million Jewish citizens of the state, or their recent ancestors, have come from 70 different countries, speaking 90 different languages. Yet within this rich ethnic mix, the Moroccan factory worker, the painter of Romanian parentage, the pop star from Yemen, the kibbutz farmer descended from early Zionist pioneers, the newly arrived American physicist, and the shopkeeper whose forebears have clung tenaciously to the place since the Middle Ages, all feel equally at home.

But this powerful sense of belonging did not happen overnight. The founders of the state realized that the transformation of newcomers from many different lands into seasoned citizens would be a complex and continuous process. Being Jewish, even being a Zionist—ideologically committed to Jewish settlement in Israel—would not be common ground enough. It would take time, effort and a subtle chemistry to imbue people from such diverse backgrounds with a shared sense of nationhood. The Jews may be an ancient people, but Israel is a young country, its first generation born into citizenship only now entering middle age.

Many different factors have been at work in the conversion of Jews into Israelis. The first is, inevitably, Zionism itself. The first Jewish settlers in Palestine, and many of their present-day successors, came to the land with the aspiration of reconstructing a Jewish state in the ancient homeland of the Hebrew people. It is hard for non-Jews, particularly those who have always been part of an ethnic majority and have never suffered persecution or discrimination, to realize the passion with which some Jews regard the opportunity of living in Israel. Yonathan Angel's view is typical of many Israelis: "A Jew can only be a proud Jew by living here." In modern Hebrew, the process of emigrating and settling in Israel is called *Aliya*, "Ascending"; new immigrants are called *olim*, "those who go up". Not all Jews are Zionists, but those who are perceive the move to Israel, quite literally, as an elevation to a higher mode of life.

Others come, not out of idealism, but in desperation. Before World War II, the last wave of immigrants to Palestine were refugees from Nazi rule. After the war, and in the first few years of Independence, the first influx of new arrivals were survivors from the Nazi Holocaust, pouring out of the Displaced Persons camps of post-war Europe. They had nowhere else to go.

Musician Rachel Kam's parents, for instance, arrived in Israel after years as refugees. Her father, uprooted from his home in southern Poland, joined a band of Russian partisans fighting the Nazis. Her blue-eyed Lithuanian-born mother saved herself from the concentration camps with a set of false papers declaring her to be of Aryan race; she spent the war years working as a housemaid in the German city of Stuttgart, terrified that her deception would be uncovered. The couple met after the war at a Displaced Persons camp in Italy, married and entered Palestine as part of a shipload of illegal immi-

3

grants defying the British blockade.

Hard on the heels of the Holocaust refugees came the mass emigrations of Jews from Arab lands. In 1949–50, 50,000 Yemenites—virtually the entire Jewish population of that country—trekked on foot or mule-back through the Arabian mountains to the British colony of Aden, where they were transported to Israel in the carefully organized airlift known as Operation Magic Carpet. A few months later Operation Ezra and Nehemiah ferried 150,000 Jews out of Iraq via Cyprus to Israel.

The 1950s and early 1960s saw a succession of lulls and peaks in the inflow of new citizens, as well as the emigration of some who had decided that the grass was, after all, greener in the lands of exile. The 1956 clash between Israel and Egypt in the Sinai peninsula brought 14,500 Egyptian Jews to Israel, while 85,000 Jewish North Afri-

cans from the newly independent and increasingly nationalist states of Morocco and Tunisia opted for *Aliya* during the same period. Refugees from political disturbances in Poland and from the 1956 Hungarian revolution swelled the numbers of European arrivals.

In the 1960s, fewer settlers came from those areas known in Israel as "the lands of stress", and more came from the affluent urban areas of North and South America, Britain and South Africa. Typical of these immigrants is Sara Ben-Menachem, Argentinian-born but now a dentist in Jerusalem. As the daughter of a prosperous industrialist her life in Buenos Aires had been comfortable. In 1961, her family sent her to Israel to fetch back a sister who, to their chagrin, wished to settle there. ("My parents were Zionists—but Zionists who did not want to live in Palestine.") As soon as she arrived, she

felt that the Jewish state, not South America, was where she belonged.

"I couldn't convince my sister to return. In fact, I liked Israel so much that I stayed myself. I felt at home here, and now Israel is my place. For better or worse..."

The Six Day War in 1967 proved a watershed. Young people from the West flocked to Israel as volunteers, to serve as army auxiliaries, construction workers, medical aides and social workers, freeing more Israelis for the war. Afterwards, many of them stayed on, spearheading another increase in immigration, and coinciding with a concerted effort by the Israeli government and the World Zionist Organization to encourage new settlement.

In the early 1970s, Israel received 45,000 Soviet Jews, the first wave of those who had struggled long and hard for permission to emigrate to Israel.

HOUSING AN INFLUX OF IMMIGRANTS

Between 1949 and 1984, about 1·75 million immigrants arrived in Israel. They came from widely different backgrounds—some were displaced persons from the refugee camps of post-war Europe, others settled from Argentina or South Africa, Iraq or Yemen. From the moment of Independence in 1948, homes had to be built in great numbers and at high speed; new villages rose rapidly, and although the buildings were often just temporary huts, they did offer lodging for tens of thousands.

Today, 40 Absorption Centres up and down the country cater for new arrivals. Here, trained staff and interpreters teach basic Hebrew, provide films and lectures on Israeli society and, above all, offer guidance on finding jobs, obtaining housing and coping with bureaucracy.

In a photograph from the 1950s, Moroccan Jews arrive at their state-built homes in Galilee.

Emigration, whatever the destination, is not a right normally accorded to any Soviet citizen; for Jews the situation has been particularly difficult. Because of their government's unfriendliness towards Israel, those who still identify as Jews are regarded with suspicion. They feel themselves to be more severely repressed than other religious or cultural minorities in the U.S.S.R. Their campaign for permission to emigrate to Israel has gained widespread sympathy in the West, although it has been only partially successful. The would-be emigrants, including many professionals and academics, cannot always afford the punitive "exit tax" imposed to recoup the state's investment in their education and training.

But not all Soviet emigrants are doctors, scientists or musicians. Thousands of members of highly religious, inward-looking Jewish communities

from Soviet Asia have also made *Aliya*, coming from Georgia, Bokhara and villages in the Caucasus mountains. Once settled in Israel, they tend to remain within their own communities, living in large extended families and preserving their own deeply pious way of life.

Soviet Jews do not all find fulfilment in the Promised Land. Once out of the U.S.S.R., some who manage to obtain exit visas settle elsewhere in the West. And a few will return to their native country, unable to adapt to an alien, non-communist environment, or disillusioned by the gap between their expectations and Israeli reality.

The 1970s and 1980s brought several thousand African newcomers: black Ethiopian Jews known as the Falashas, the "Strangers". They are thought by some scholars to have derived from the ancient Israelite tribe of Dan. Living in remote mountainous regions, they

were completely cut off from the Jewish mainstream; indeed, until the end of the 19th century, they believed that all Jews were black. They retained customs that the rest of the Jewish world had long abandoned, such as animal sacrifice, and used an ancient Ethiopic dialect instead of Hebrew as their liturgical language. Although they possessed the Torah—the Five Books of Moses—they had no knowledge of later religious texts such as the Talmud.

When Ethiopia was devastated by famine in the early 1980s, the trickle of Ethiopians turned into a well-publicized flood. Some 7,500 were evacuated to Israel in 1984 by a covert and politically controversial airlift called Operation Moses. Nations unfriendly to Israel condemned it as a political propaganda ploy, while Israelis defended their action as a bold attempt to rescue their people from a war-torn land that could no longer feed them.

"We can only gain from showing the world the extent to which we are willing to go to rescue Jews," said one Israeli government official. "This mission is a national achievement of the highest order."

In a world where many states are keen to restrict immigration by re-writing their laws and devising legal loopholes to keep people out, Israel may well be unique in its efforts to encourage and assist new arrivals. There is, however, a crucial condition: Israel's doors are open, but only Jews have the automatic right to Israeli citizenship. The 1948 Declaration of Independence proclaimed: "The State of Israel shall be open to Jewish immigration and the ingathering of the exiles." Two years after Independence, the Knesset, Israel's Parliament, passed the 1950 Law

The director of a Beersheba absorption centre stops for a chat with Ethiopian newcomers.

3

of Return, granting every Jew the right of permanent settlement in Israel, followed in 1954 by a statute entitling all Jewish immigrants to citizenship as soon as they set foot on Israeli soil.

This Right of Return continues to generate controversies. According to religious law, a person may be defined as a Jew if he or she is the child of a Jewish mother, or a convert who has adopted Judaism after a prescribed course of study and a ritual conversion process carried out by a rabbi. But a small and vocal minority within the Israeli religious establishment question the identity of groups such as the Ethiopians, whose origins and traditions differ from those of other Jews. It was not until 1973, after much acrimonious debate over the first Ethiopian arrivals, that they were officially acknowledged as Jews by the religious establishment. Some rabbis demanded they undergo a form of symbolic conversion ceremony to confirm their Jewishness. Not surprisingly, the Ethiopians, who feel their own ritual purity far exceeds that of most Israelis, indignantly refused.

Non-Jews may also apply for naturalization, but they have no automatic entitlement to citizenship. Even some members of the Jewish faith no longer enjoy the undisputed right to an Israeli passport. It was discovered that certain Jewish criminals, or those with strong underworld associations, experienced sudden bursts of Zionist fervour when they felt the hot breath of the law on their necks. In 1972, for instance, New Yorker Meyer Lansky, worried by the attentions of an American grand jury, was denied the right of permanent residence in Israel. His unsuccessful lawsuit against the government was one of a number of test cases, reinforcing the Minister of the Interior's right to withhold an immigrant's visa from "a person with a criminal past, likely to endanger the public welfare".

For more law-abiding citizens who wish to move to Israel, the path is made smoother by the Jewish Agency of the autonomous World Zionist Organization. The Agency maintains offices in countries with substantial Jewish populations, staffed by Israeli counsellors—*shlichim*, literally "messengers"—who provide guidance and help for prospective immigrants.

In some cases, several like-minded people will decide to emigrate together. A group of young Americans or Canadians, for instance, with a common philosophy of life and shared political or religious opinions, will form a *garin*—a settlement group of perhaps 10 families—and pool their resources to establish a new kibbutz. They will negotiate with the Ministry of the Interior for permission to settle in an undeveloped area, and live in caravans until permanent dwellings can be built. Or a party of engineers and scientists may decide to create a new community within commuting distance of Israel's high technology industries.

More often, however, individuals come to Israel singly or in families, and spend their first few months in the Jewish Agency's residential hostels and Absorption Centres. Here they study the Hebrew language and acclimatize themselves to life in a new country. Trained staff are on hand to assist them in job and house-hunting, and to guide them through the labyrinths of the Israeli bureaucracy. It takes patience, persistence and a level head to acquire identity cards, health insurance and the numerous tax concessions and benefits available only to newcomers; civil servants operate an intricate system

81

3

that retains elements of imperial Ottoman law and British Mandatory practices, with newer Israeli regulations grafted on top.

Zionism may provide the impetus for settlement and the absorption services may offer newcomers the resources to make themselves at home in their adopted country, but since the very beginning of the state there has been no agency as powerful as the Israeli Defence Forces for turning immigrants into Israelis. All new residents, male and female, are liable for conscription under the same terms and conditions as native-born Israelis.

Because the nation was born out of war, the first immigrants to the newly established nation had little option but to join in the collective battle for survival. During the 1948–49 War of Independence all hands were needed, and it was not unknown for an immigrant to become an Israeli citizen and an Israeli casualty on the same day. But once the war was over, the founders of the nation felt it was possible for the army to play a more pacific and constructive role. "The army," observed David Ben-Gurion, "is obliged to become the creative force of the nation's pioneers, and the cultural instrument for the assimilation of returnees, for their integration and their advancement."

The Defence Service Law of 1949 established the foundation for the key educational role of the military establishment. Under the terms of this law, the army was mandated to teach conscripts the Hebrew language, Bible studies, Israeli and general history, geography, science and other disciplines. Today its three-month courses in these subjects, equipped with special textbooks, provide an intensive 200 hours of tuition aimed at bringing every recruit up to the minimum basic educational standard. It is probably the only military organization in the world that has won a national prize for contributions to education.

By Western standards, Israel's army is unconventional in many other ways. Enlisted men and women are often on familiar first-name terms with their officers, they share the same rations and eat in the same mess, and—in times of peace at least—they feel free to argue with their superiors rather than obey orders unquestioningly.

Women in the army perform a wide range of non-combat roles but, to the frustration of some female soldiers, they are no longer sent to the front lines. Indeed, Israeli feminists have pointed out that although women and men are equally liable to conscription, women have more opportunities to avoid their military service and—if enlisted—are more restricted in their choice of role than their counterparts, for instance, in the U.S. army. However, women soldiers are trained for combat so that they can be used extensively as technical instructors. It is common on Israeli military bases to see 19-year-old female sergeants drilling a platoon of reservists old enough to be their fathers, and to see equally youthful women officers teaching conscripts to use machine guns or drive tanks.

Both women and men are trained with equal rigour for the élite units of the Nahal. Nahal—a Hebrew acronym for Fighting Pioneer Youth—is a division of the Israeli Defence Forces with the mission of forming and maintaining armed agricultural settlements and kibbutzim in the sensitive border areas. Its members are instructed in the skills of farming as well as fighting, and spend their enlisted time living and working in these communities.

Most Israelis look upon their military service as an obligation to the community. But there are, as in every country, those who would prefer to avoid conscription. Women are exempted from service if they are married or if they declare themselves to be highly religious; it is accepted that the traditional codes of dress and conduct for a pious Jewish woman are incompatible with the demands of military life. However, one young woman who had obtained an exemption on grounds of her extreme piety was spotted a week later taking part in the Miss Tel Aviv contest, clad in the briefest of bikinis; she was instantly hustled into the army.

The Israeli man without a military record carries a stigma for the rest of his life, so some young men go to extreme lengths to gain entry. A military doctor in Jerusalem remarked that "we are probably the only army medics in the world who find ourselves trying to detect sick boys who claim to be healthy, rather than the other way around".

Yudin Ya'akov, a young would-be recruit, was turned down by the IDF because of poor hearing. Since his disability was not apparent, he became the subject of malicious gossip among his neighbours, who accused him of shirking his duties. Frustrated, Ya'akov sued the army, claiming that his impaired hearing did not make him unfit for service, and that his rejection had caused him "unjustifiable shame and brought disgrace" upon his family. The Supreme Court upheld his claim ordering that he be inducted at once.

In spite of its risks and perils, military service brings concrete rewards to the veteran, providing specialist qualifications, financial benefits and an en-

In a quiet corner of Jerusalem's Mea Shearim district, a resident emerges into a street festooned with laundry. Founded in 1874 by ultra-orthodox Jews, the quarter preserves something of the atmosphere of Eastern Europe's vanished ghettoes.

ormous pool of social and professional contacts. In the army, Israelis of different ethnic backgrounds, generations and social classes get to know one another; barriers of ignorance and prejudice are inevitably broken down. Because the IDF touches the lives of the overwhelming majority—native-born and newcomers alike—it may well be the one Israeli institution that can truly claim to be a "melting pot".

After only decades of Independence, Israel is still a nation in flux, a society very much in its infancy. Without the inheritance of a continuous common culture and a shared history, played out in a single place, Israelis are engrossed in the process of inventing and defining their own national identity.

The Hebrew language, adapted by Zionist scholars for modern use, has been a cohesive force. Once immigrants have learnt the language, they often express a desire for assimilation by changing their names into something that sounds more Hebraic. It is probably easier to legally change a name in Israel than anywhere else, and 80 per cent of Israelis have seen fit to do so. By filling in a short form and paying a nominal fee at a government office, a citizen is instantly transformed. Within minutes, a woman with the Arabic-Jewish name of Toria Sa'id, for instance, becomes the far more Israeli-sounding Nurit Shimoni.

The precedent for this was set long before Independence: the early Zionist settlers felt it was one way of proving their resolve to build new lives in a new country. A young Russian Jew named David Grien, for instance, emigrated to Palestine and became David Ben-Gurion. Succeeding prime ministers have done the same: Moshe Shertok

In a religious ecstasy, members of the Hasidic sect swirl inside a Mea Shearim synagogue while one of their number claps out a rhythm. The circular dance symbolizes a Hasidic precept: no-one leads, no-one follows, all are equal before God.

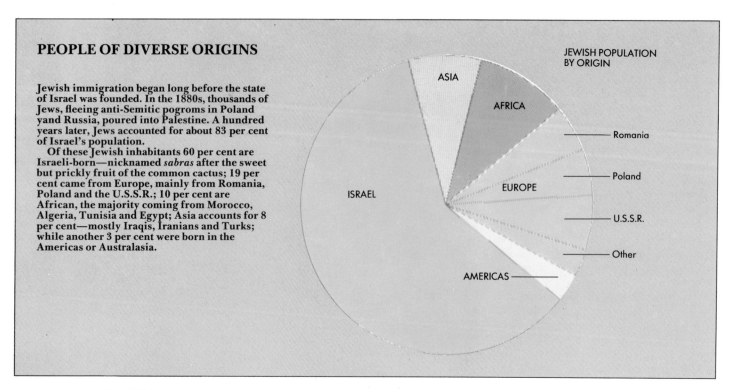

PEOPLE OF DIVERSE ORIGINS

Jewish immigration began long before the state of Israel was founded. In the 1880s, thousands of Jews, fleeing anti-Semitic pogroms in Poland yand Russia, poured into Palestine. A hundred years later, Jews accounted for about 83 per cent of Israel's population.

Of these Jewish inhabitants 60 per cent are Israeli-born—nicknamed *sabras* after the sweet but prickly fruit of the common cactus; 19 per cent came from Europe, mainly from Romania, Poland and the U.S.S.R.; 10 per cent are African, the majority coming from Morocco, Algeria, Tunisia and Egypt; Asia accounts for 8 per cent—mostly Iraqis, Iranians and Turks; while another 3 per cent were born in the Americas or Australasia.

JEWISH POPULATION BY ORIGIN

ASIA
AFRICA
Romania
Poland
EUROPE
U.S.S.R.
ISRAEL
Other
AMERICAS

became Sharett, Levi Shkolnick became Levi Eshkol, Golda Myerson opted for the more Hebraic surname of Meir.

Just as individuals take new names to reflect their new nationality, so the Israeli authorities have created new place names to put a Hebrew stamp on the map. In part, the creation of new names reflects the creation of new places: some 1,000 kibbutzim, villages and development towns have been established since the first waves of Zionist settlement, 650 since Independence. A Names Committee, composed of specialists in archaeology, history, geography, folklore and ancient Hebrew, meets regularly to consider names for these fledgling communities.

First set up in 1924 by the Jewish Agency, the committee became a gov-

ernment body after statehood. It has named more than 889 locations, often reviving place names mentioned in the Bible or the Talmud.

A new settlement in the Hebron hills, for instance, was named Othniel, after one of the judges who presided over the tribes of Israel in the time of Joshua—12th century B.C.—who was known to have lived in the district.

Even when the scriptures supply no specific geographical or historical association, they may still be used as sources of inspiration. Faced with the task of naming a cluster of three rural villages in the northern Negev and the new town that would serve them as a regional centre, the committee looked to a verse in Isaiah 41:19: "I will plant in the wilderness . . . the fig tree, and the

pine and the box tree, together." The villages were called by the Hebrew words for the trees—Berosh, Tidhar and Ta'ashur—while the central town was named Yahdav ("Together").

Other new communities have more recent associations. The committee has named settlements after figures from modern Jewish history—Herzliyya, for example, commemorates the founding father of Zionism, Theodor Herzl—and after military heroes: a Jordan Valley settlement Netiv Halamed-heh ("The Thirty-Five") perpetuates the memory of 35 soldiers who fell there. Non-Jewish supporters of the state are similarly honoured: the kibbutz of Ramat David for the former British prime minister David Lloyd George, an early supporter of the Zionist cause, and

Kfar Truman for the American president who urged the United Nations to approve an independent Israeli state.

"Instead of erecting a statue in the park," explained one committee member, "we prefer to award friends of our nation a living memorial, and name a settlement after them."

It is not surprising that a state whose claim to its territory is still questioned by some should be so zealous in reinforcing its people's long-standing connection with the land. But this concern is practical as well as political. Older nations take their heroes, legends and patriotic symbols for granted, as part of their cultural heritage, but a new society needs to invent them afresh.

For the so-called "People of the Book" it is natural that the Bible

should be the principal source for this imagery. During his term as Israel's first prime minister, David Ben-Gurion insisted that the study of the Bible—as geography, history and literature rather than as holy writ—be made an integral part of the school curriculum, to give the rising generation a positive Jewish-Israeli identity.

For the same reason, objects from Jewish history were chosen as national symbols. The six-pointed star known as the Shield of David was placed on the Israeli flag, and the Menora—a seven-branched candelabra revered as a reminder of the ancient temple—became the official state emblem and the insignia of the Israeli Defence Forces.

Places also take on symbolic significance. The Western Wall in Jerusalem

is the sole surviving remnant of the Second Temple and a site charged with a sense of history and national sentiment. So, too, is Masada, on its lonely rock in the Judaean desert. Here, where 960 Jewish resistance fighters, men, women and children, committed suicide in 73 A.D. rather than yield to Roman besiegers, new recruits to the IDF's élite Armoured Corps take their oath of allegiance, vowing that "Masada shall not fall again".

Horrors more recent than a Roman siege have burnt the promise "Never Again" even deeper into the Israeli soul. The sombre monument of Yad Vashem (the name means "hand" and "name") in Jerusalem is dedicated to the six million Jews who died at Nazi hands, over one third of the world's

3

Jewish population at the time. Here, historical archives—photographic records of concentration camp atrocities and memorial plaques to European Jewish communities that were wiped out—are preserved to ensure Israelis never forget, never grow complacent.

The Holocaust has profound implications for all Israelis, whether of European or Afro-Asian origin. But after 2,000 years of dispersion, Jews from different regions have different histories; they are no longer, if they ever were, one homogeneous ethnic group.

Relations between Ashkenazi Jews, who originate in the Yiddish-speaking communities of Central and Eastern Europe, and Jews of Oriental and North African extraction have not always been easy. The latter are known, imprecisely, as Sephardim, after Sepharad—the ancient Hebrew name for Spain. Strictly speaking, Sephardim are those who can trace their ancestry back to the large Jewish communities that flourished in Spain during the Middle Ages, but in Israeli parlance the term is often used to distinguish those Jews who are of Afro-Asian as opposed to "European" stock.

When the state was first founded, the Ashkenazim were in the majority. Now, after waves of immigration from the Arab world and a consistently higher birth rate, the Sephardim form just over half of the Jewish population.

Each group has its rich and poor, its proletarians, peasants and urban cosmopolites. But for the first three decades of the state's existence, Jews from North Africa and Yemen—who came from economically and educationally deprived backgrounds—clustered in the most underprivileged sectors of Israeli society. Despite its egalitarian

ideals, the nation appeared, for a time, to be moving towards an ethnically based class system.

From the beginning, Ashkenazi Jews were firmly in control of the establishment, occupying the prime jobs, enjoying the best housing and running the government. Many Afro-Asian immigrants remained at the bottom of the ladder, living in slums and working in poorly paid menial jobs. Because of their higher birth rate, they suffered disproportionately from overcrowded and inadequate housing. In schools, their children often displayed the problems associated with a background of poverty and multiple deprivation: they failed more subjects, dropped out of school earlier, and fell into petty crime at a rate far greater than their more privileged European contemporaries.

Inevitably, frustration in these communities mounted. In 1971, a group of young Jews of Middle-Eastern origin, angry at what they saw as official indifference to their plight, formed a protest movement. They named it the Black Panthers, drawing a parallel between their own struggle and that of black militants in the U.S. They staged angry and sometimes violent demonstrations in the cities; some were jailed. Prime Minister Golda Meir, after receiving an angry delegation of them in 1972, sent them away with the remark, "These are not nice boys."

But the government was not complacent. The Ministry of Education instituted policies to integrate poor and middle-class school children, to break the vicious circle of deprived children in deprived schools in deprived neighbourhoods. The package of education reforms and financial assistance included grants to aid large families, provision of extra tutoring and the creation

On the beachfront of Tel Aviv, within sight of the city's marina, Israelis stroll along the decorative promenade of Hayarkon Street, sunbathe, or swim in the Mediterranean Sea. In front of one of the blue and white changing booths *(inset)*, an elderly man rubs suntan oil into a friend's back.

3

of remedial and enrichment programmes to improve students' chances of qualifying for higher education.

The state has also poured massive resources into welfare services and housing, while Israel's central trade union organization, the Histadrut, has guaranteed all workers the right to equal pay and promotion prospects. Economic inequities and housing problems take time to rectify, but the gulf does appear to be narrowing at last.

Material improvements do not automatically put paid to inter-communal tensions. Many Israelis of Afro-Asian origin feel that they have been written out of the nation's history.

In schools, for instance, they complain that little is said about those settlers who came from Yemen or Iraq at the same time as the early Zionist pioneers from Central and Eastern Europe. Because the latter were politically and culturally dominant, they tended to forget that Afro-Asian Jews had also played a role. "They teach that 'the first *Aliya* was this group, the second *Aliya* was that group'—but where are the Sephardim?" asks one Yemenite university lecturer, a specialist on Jews from Islamic countries.

A North African community leader feels that it is time his own people were appreciated as contributors to Israeli life—not merely as stereotyped purveyors of exotic delicacies or the wearers of picturesque costume. "We want to be recognized not via the couscous and the caftan, but through our writers and poets, through our agricultural achievements and through our willingness to sacrifice ourselves in the line of fire on the nation's borders."

For many Israelis the goal now is to achieve a society that is, at once, heterogeneous and united, ethnically var-

KOSHER FOOD LAWS

A rabbi holds up a scoop of kosher flour.

The dietary laws of *kashrut* (Hebrew for "right" or "fit"), dictating the food that Jews may or may not eat, originated in the Old Testament. For the citizen of modern Israel, whether to eat kosher or not is a personal matter, but many people do observe the prohibitions against shellfish, pork and certain other meats, and refrain from mixing meat and dairy foods.

Some firms employ rabbis to ensure that their products conform to the minutely detailed rules of *kashrut*. Flour mills, for example, seek confirmation that the meal used in the making of Passover *matzoth*—unleavened bread—has not fermented.

ied but socially equal. Educational and cultural organizations such as Beyahad ("Together") work towards this end. Founded by North Africans in 1979, it seeks not only to celebrate the contributions made by Afro-Asian Jewry, but to encourage tolerance and mutual appreciation between all Israelis—Oriental and European, Jew and Arab.

One of the most successful of its projects has been the expansion of the traditional North African Jewish spring holiday, Mimouna, into a national celebration. Customarily, North African families treat this two-day festival as an occasion for impromptu, but lavish, hospitality. They open their houses to all their neighbours, offering traditional sweetmeats and mint tea. Under the auspices of Beyahad, Mimouna has become a large-scale public event with vast communal picnics and folk festivals in the parks, open-air exhibitions celebrating the nation's cultural diversity, ceremonial visits by public figures to North African households and an officially sanctioned day off school. The organizers see the occasion as an opportunity for Israelis of many different backgrounds to begin to understand each other, a way to break down prejudices that still survive.

"We haven't yet reached the stage of respecting one another's cultures," admits founder, Sam Ben-Chetrit. But he is optimistic: "Israeli society is more open today than before, more tolerant and prepared to listen. There is a readiness to solve problems."

With increasing frequency, different cultures meet within one household, as the children of immigrants intermarry. One family where two worlds converge is that of Yonathan and Eliana Angel, who live on the northern edge of the

Negev, in the town of Sederot.

The Angels' family history is itself an example of the Zionist act of "gathering in the exiles". Both Yonathan and Eliana were born in Israel, but grew up in two different environments: Yonathan is a Yemenite-Israeli, Eliana's origins are Polish.

Yonathan—also known as Natti—is olive-skinned, slim, slightly balding. He has a finely sculptured Yemenite face, burning black eyes and slender hands. He wears colourful turtle-neck sweaters and jeans, and never puts on a tie. He speaks in the rhythmic, authentic Hebrew that the Yemenites have preserved since they were exiled from Palestine 2,000 years ago. His father

came to Israel as a child, in 1903, as part of the Yemenites' own *Aliya*. The family spent six months on an arduous trek, sometimes riding on donkeys, sometimes on foot, to reach the Red Sea port of Aden. Here they found a boat bound for Palestine. On the journey, the small boy was entrusted with the family's most precious Yemenite heirloom—a magnificent antique silver water-pipe, standing one metre high—which today adorns the Angels' comfortable sitting-room in Sederot.

Natti himself was born in the city of Petah Tikvah, north of Tel Aviv. He remembers that his father walked great distances every day to labour in the citrus plantations outside the city, and

that his mother took in laundry to help support the large family.

Following the pattern of many of his contemporaries from deprived backgrounds, Natti dropped out of school in his early teens. He had little ambition or sense of direction. "I was a ne'er-do-well until I met Eliana," he admits.

Fair-skinned, round-faced Eliana Zaidengart comes from another world. She is, like so many Ashkenazim of her generation, a child of the Holocaust: her medical student father was shipped off to a concentration camp; her mother endured three nightmarish years at Auschwitz. Eliana was born in the port of Jaffa (now part of the municipality of Tel Aviv-Jaffa). In her early teens she

3

moved with her family to Sederot, then a struggling frontier settlement.

When Eliana went back to Tel Aviv to train as a teacher, she met and married Natti, and persuaded him to return with her to Sederot. At first, he found the place too quiet.

"I had a hard time adjusting. I was a city boy and here I was cooped up in a village. But I've grown to love it here. We have a closely knit group of friends of our own age—Yemenites, Tunisians, Poles. The tempo is relaxed, and I'm doing well at the plant."

Natti works in a pharmaceuticals factory, making bandages and other surgical products from the locally-grown cotton. Eliana teaches kindergarten and runs a cultural enrichment programme for the local schools.

Natti identifies himself as a Yemenite-Israeli and Eliana sees herself as a Polish-Israeli, but their three sons are unmistakably *sabras*—native-born Israeli citizens nicknamed after the indigenous cactus that is prickly outside, but soft and sweet within.

"It never occurs to them or to their friends to question whether they are Ashkenazi or Sephardi," says Eliana. Her husband agrees, and insists that the children feel no discrimination because their skin is darker or because their father is a Yemenite. "Even I personally did not feel it in my youth, although I realized that the country then was being run by Europeans, and it is natural for the ruling group to favour its own. We all do that—Ashkenazi or Sephardi or Yemenite. Gaps really come from cultural differences. As soon as they are bridged, the gaps disappear. That is one Israeli problem that doesn't worry me."

Sederot, where the Angels live, is one of Israel's 30 development towns, a

meeting place for many different immigrant groups. It was established in 1954 as part of a programme of planned settlements. They were intended to distribute the burgeoning population over a wider area, and to provide a commercial and industrial base for the growing number of kibbutzim and agricultural co-operatives. Sederot, for instance, has several plants making use of local crops: a cotton gin, the pharmaceuticals firm where Natti Angel works, a poultry-processing factory and a potato crisp manufacturer.

The town's first inhabitants were immigrants from Iraq, Iran and Kurdistan, joined later by Eastern Europeans, North Africans and—even more recently—by Ethiopians.

In the early days, Sederot, like most development towns, was a spartan place, composed mostly of temporary huts and cabins where large families squeezed into one or two small rooms. But these have gradually been replaced by new houses—built mainly by the Arab labourers who commute from Gaza, 20 kilometres away.

Sephardi Jews, who form the major-

ity in the development town, are traditionally very pious; Sederot boasts 20 synagogues, for a population of 10,000, as well as social clubs, shops and a cinema showing first-run European and American films. Buses go to Tel Aviv and Beersheba, a two-hour journey, but there is no local public transport. People without cars use bicycles or horses, or simply walk. Despite light industries and a polyglot population, Sederot remains a small country town, without a single traffic light.

The pace of life outside semi-rural Sederot is more frenetic. Eighty-five per cent of the population are urbanites, most living on the crowded coastal plain: Greater Tel Aviv alone houses 35 per cent of the population.

In many ways, the lifestyles of these Israelis do not differ markedly from those of their counterparts elsewhere. But demographically as well as geographically, they are poised between two worlds, not quite a Middle Eastern society, not quite European.

This mingling of cultures is reflected in their favourite pastimes and sports.

At a kibbutz near Caesarea, young basketball enthusiasts practise blocking and passing. The sport's popularity skyrocketed when an Israeli team, Maccabi Tel Aviv, achieved international fame by winning a series of European championships.

Intent on perfection, Isaac Stern rehearses for a concert. The violinist has long been a patron of Israeli efforts to nurture budding talent through prizes, scholarships and Young Artists' Weeks, when youthful musicians receive widespread national attention.

As befits a land with so benign a climate, these pleasures are often taken out of doors. As in other Mediterranean countries, people are forever eating in the streets; food-vendors offer everything from Middle Eastern chickpea fritters to transatlantic hot-dogs, and discarded shells of sunflower seeds—a favourite snack—crackle underfoot.

The most popular sports mirror this diversity: soccer is supported as fanatically in Israel as anywhere in Europe, and an important national match can bring the country virtually to a halt. North American immigrants have imported their devotion to basketball, which has been embraced enthusiastically throughout Israel; one shining star has been a black American convert to Judaism. And the erstwhile British Empire has sent cricketers: Australians, Englishmen and Indians.

Popular culture provides the context for other forms of cross-fertilization. The Hebrew-language songs at the top of the pop music charts, for example, amalgamate Arabic, Latin and North American styles. In one respect, Israelis perpetuate the cultural values of the lost world of Central-European Jewry: they are passionate devotees of classical music. Israel has a higher percentage of concert-goers than any other country, and takes pride in the success of such native sons as violinists Yitzhak Perlman and Pinchas Zukerman, and conductor Daniel Barenboim.

Young musicians and other performing artists are carefully nurtured by means of special tutoring, scholarships and youth orchestras. In so small a country, efforts can be made to prevent talent from slipping through the net, even if it sometimes means that the rules must be bent a little: "I will not let the army stand in the way of this girl's career as a dancer!" one IDF officer was heard to say, as she ordered a young conscript to go off from guard duty in time for rehearsal.

For viola player Rachel Kam, a place in the Israel Philharmonic Orchestra was the pinnacle of her musical ambition. "For an Israeli kid, the Philharmonic was untouchable."

Thanks to sympathetic teaching, and a scholarship from the same cultural foundation that launched Yitzhak Perlman and Pinchas Zukerman on their careers, she eventually won a place in the orchestra. Now she fits in family life around the IPO's punishing concert schedule—around 300 concerts a year, and foreign tours as far afield as South America and Japan. "We are always well-received," she says. "I think the IPO is one of Israel's best ambassadors."

The orchestra's distinguished international reputation is, for all Israelis, a matter of patriotic pride. As citizens of a small, young and much-criticized country, they display an almost obsessive need to excel at everything they do.

Yet simpler, more pragmatic hopes for the future go hand in hand with these vaulting ambitions. "I look at my kids," says Rachel Kam, "and I wish for them to be happy in Israel and not to have to fight any more wars, to be content with themselves, and to get the best out of every working day."

WITHIN THE WALLS
OF OLD JERUSALEM

Crammed into a scant square kilometre and enclosed by its massive 16th-century walls, the Old City of Jerusalem has a unique importance for three of the world's major religions: among its jumbled buildings and labyrinthine alleys lie some of the oldest and holiest shrines of each faith.

The Old City, which occupies less than one per cent of Israel's sprawling capital, consists of four sectors. Built on the spacious platform that was once the site of Solomon's temple, the Dome of the Rock—Islam's oldest surviving religious monument—rises above the Muslim Quarter. The platform's western revetment is the Western Wall—ancient focus of exiled Jewry's longing for Jerusalem—which now forms one boundary of the Jewish Quarter. The Christian Quarter surrounds the site of Christ's death and burial, while the small Armenian Quarter harbours a Christian community which has dwelt in the same spot for 1,600 years.

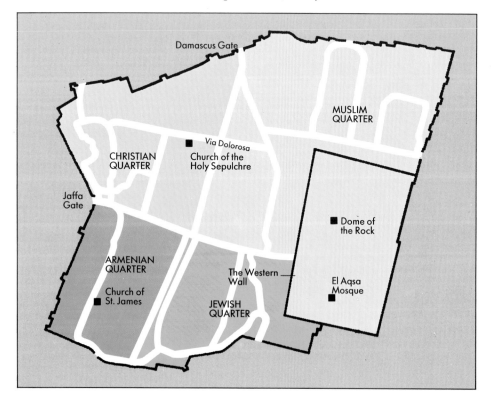

The map shows the approximate boundaries of the four quarters, together with the major religious monuments and important streets. In the maze of lanes, the churches, synagogues and mosques jostle for space with ordinary dwellings.

In the Muslim Quarter of the Old City,
television aerials surmount limestone
houses built in a style that has hardly
changed over the centuries. Jerusalem's
centre has probably been inhabited
continuously for 4,000 years.

A customer at one of the many cafés in the crowded Muslim Quarter smokes a hookah with a glass of mint tea at his elbow. Each establishment has its faithful habitués—Arab men who regard the place as a second home.

Men gather for Friday-morning prayers before the ornate façade of the Dome of the Rock, the majestic mosque built in 691 A.D. and redecorated in the 16th century. It stands on one of Islam's holiest places: the rock from which Muhammad was taken up to heaven.

In the medieval covered market in the Muslim Quarter, where the Old City's commercial life is concentrated, a trader sweeps the pavement in front of his lamplit vegetable stall. The Muslim market's busiest time is on Saturday, the Jewish Sabbath, when all the Jewish shops are shut.

In a square of the Armenian Quarter, members of a family gather outside their house. The quarter—with some buildings dating back to the time of the Crusades—is a city within a city, enclosed by thick walls. Many of its residents earn their living by making jewellery.

96

Observed by a cowled monk, a young seminarian at the Armenian cathedral of St. James beats a wooden sounding board. The board, and the metal one beside it, have summoned worshippers to prayer since the 16th century, when Ottoman rulers forbade bell-ringing.

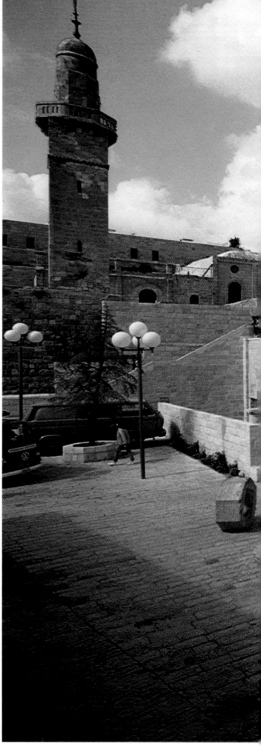

Refuse collectors in one of the narrow alleys of the Jewish Quarter *(left)* perch on their vehicle to let a pedestrian edge past. Although the Muslim Quarter is the largest, the Jewish population of the Old City now outnumbers that of the other three quarters.

Children dash across the Hurva Square *(right)*, one of the Jewish Quarter's carefully renovated areas. Since 1967, when Israel reclaimed those parts of the city previously held by Jordan, the quarter has seen an ambitious programme of rebuilding.

Ethiopian monks sit reading outside their cell-like rooms above the Church of the Holy Sepulchre, the Christian Quarter's holiest shrine. Since the 19th century, when they were banished by rival sects from the building, the Ethiopians have laid claim to the roof.

On the sunlit steps of the Holy Sepulchre, two Christian Arabs polish a pair of giant candlesticks. Most of the people in the Christian Quarter are of Arab extraction, educated in Christian schools. Since 1948, the Christian population of the Old City has fallen from about 25,000 to 10,000.

THE CHRISTIAN QUARTER

Franciscan monks lead a procession of pilgrims along the Via Dolorosa, the Street of Sorrows, the route Jesus is believed to have followed to Calvary. Starting from the temple esplanade, the way passes through the Muslim Quarter and finishes at the Church of the Holy Sepulchre.

4

COEXISTING
WITH MINORITIES

A veiled Palestinian Arab woman
peeps out from her shop in a village
near Hebron on the West Bank. About
800,000 Palestinian Arabs live in this
territory, which was occupied by Israel
in 1967. More than half a million other
Arabs within Israel's pre-1967 borders
are fully fledged citizens of the state.

The Declaration of Independence, issued by Israel's founders on the eve of
statehood, proclaimed the right of the
Jewish people to national revival in the
land which was the birthplace of their
faith. Recalling the Diaspora, the early
struggles of Zionism and the horrors of
the Holocaust, it also set out the ideals
upon which the state was to be based.
Israel, it asserted, would uphold "the
full social and political equality of all its
citizens without distinction of religion,
race or sex" and, it continued, "in the
midst of wanton aggression, we yet call
upon the Arab inhabitants of the State
of Israel to preserve the ways of peace
and play their part in the development
of the State, on the basis of full and
equal citizenship . . ."

In its short existence, Israel has had a
remarkable record of making some of
its ideals work in practice. It has, for
example, been conspicuously successful in welding a nation from the disparate elements of its Jewish population.
But integrating its Arab inhabitants
has proved a much more painful and
perplexing problem. Israel has yet to
resolve the apparent contradiction of
preserving itself as a Jewish homeland
while at the same time aspiring to be a
secular democracy with equal rights for
all its citizens, Jew and Arab alike.

One out of every seven Israeli citizens—some 600,000 out of a total population of 4.3 million—is an Arab.
Outside the state's internationally recognized borders, but within the areas

occupied since the 1967 war, live nearly
1.4 million other Arabs—111,000 in
the part of Jerusalem formerly held by
Jordan, 800,000 outside the city in the
territory that Israelis call Judaea and
Samaria but the rest of the world knows
as the West Bank, and 450,000 in Gaza.

These territories are ruled by a military administration and their Arab residents do not have Israeli citizenship.
Their status and future pose questions
that must be resolved in the search for
lasting peace in the Middle East.

Until this peace is achieved, Arab
citizens of the state of Israel remain in a
difficult position. Whatever their political views, they are, ethnically and re-
ligiously, closer kin to their country's
enemies than they are to their Jewish
fellow-citizens. But to generalize about
the Arabs is as impossible as it is to
do so about the Jews. Culturally, re-
ligiously and economically, Israeli
Arabs are anything but homogeneous.
The prosperous, Westernized Arab
businessman or the politically radical
university student have more in common with their Jewish-Israeli counterparts than they do with each other. And
both feel equally alien to the Bedouin
shepherd, dwelling in his carpeted tent.

In religion, the Arab population is
surprisingly diverse. About 75 per cent
are Muslims, while another 14 per cent
profess Christianity, most as Greek
Catholics—affiliated to Rome—or as
Greek Orthodox communicants; many
are descended from Arabs converted

103

4

On the misty summit of Mount
Gerizim, a sacred site of Israel's 550
Samaritans, a priest celebrates their
version of the Jewish feast of Passover.
Last remnants of a separate sect that
emerged in the fifth century B.C., they
believe that they alone are the true
spiritual heirs of the Tribes of Israel.

by the European missionaries during the Crusades. And defining themselves as neither Christian nor Muslim are 47,000 Druze, members of a self-contained religion which split from Islam in the 11th century. The Druze dogma is jealously guarded, known only to an élite within their own tightly knit community, which is scattered throughout the mountainous regions of Syria, Lebanon and northern Israel.

The Druze in Israel have always believed that co-operation with the Jews was in their own best interests; they are the only Israeli Arabs who, at the request of their leaders, do compulsory service in the Israeli Defence Forces: the only exceptions are the 15,000 Druze of the Golan Heights, formerly Syrian subjects, who remained neutral during the fighting with Syria in 1973. Famous for their bravery, many Druze soldiers go on to careers in the frontier police, patrolling the northern borders.

All other Arab citizens are exempted from military service. It would put Israeli Arabs in an impossible moral position, say Israeli authorities, if they were asked to fight against other Arabs from hostile states. The Jewish-Israeli man-in-the-street does not always appreciate the finer points of this dilemma: "Until they do national service, like we do," flatly declares one Jerusalemite, "they cannot be equal."

Arabs, too, regard this exclusion as an indication of their status as second-class citizens. They may appreciate the freedom from conscription and long rounds of reserve duty, but they pay a price; anyone who does not serve in the military forces misses out on the elaborate system of benefits—grants, scholarships, mortgage assistance and other financial aid—designed to compensate Israeli citizen-soldiers for the time they lose in their civilian careers.

Throughout the state, Arabs and Jews still reside mainly in separate communities. In the countryside, Arab villages lie apart from Jewish settlements; in the cities, Arabs occupy different neighbourhoods. There are, for instance, sizeable Arab minorities in Jaffa, Haifa and Acre. Jaffa, once Palestine's principal port and the landing place of centuries of Holy Land pilgrims, has now been absorbed into the larger city of Tel Aviv. Here, an estimated 15,000 Arabs are crowded into the slum streets of the Ajami and Jabalyeh quarters, whose squalor contrasts with the modern, if monotonous, Jewish housing blocks nearby. Jaffa's Arabs work mostly for small private contractors—Jewish, Christian or Muslim—who hire them, often by the day, for unskilled work in building, street-cleaning, dishwashing or agriculture. Israeli newspapers such as the liberal daily *Ha'eretz* have campaigned repeatedly for the Jaffa Arabs to be rehoused, with little result.

In Haifa, the picture is different. This port town, as it climbs up Mount Carmel, has an air of almost Germanic solidity, and its Arab minority includes a number of wealthy merchants and contractors. At rush hours, buses are crowded with Arab workers heading for the industrial area around Haifa Bay, and Arab students bound for the University or for Israel's élite scientific institute, the Technion. Above the city, in the Carmel mountains, prosperous farmers and small businessmen reside in trim, well-kept Druze villages. Their houses display an unusual preference for windows of all shapes and sizes, often on the same façade.

Farther north, surrounded by palms, lies the walled town of Acre, now a

CONTRASTING ARAB LIFESTYLES

As is clear from their lifestyles, religions and political attitudes, Israeli Arabs are far from being a homogeneous community. The Druze, for example, who belong to a secret religion which broke from Islam in the 11th century, have integrated themselves thoroughly. Many Muslim Palestinians, in contrast, oppose Israeli rule, while their co-religionists, the Bedouin, cling to a lifestyle that has little to do with modern political exigencies.

Yet these groups are linked by common cultural traits. Their homes, for example—be they tents or concrete villas—are furnished in a similar style, and their women withdraw when male guests arrive.

Wearing the hat and scarf that mark him as an initiate in the mysteries of his sect, a Druze elder *(right)* stands at his door. His "welcoming room" *(below)* is furnished with Western seats and a variety of rugs and colourful cushions spread on the floor for Arab visitors.

In the living room of their three-room house, a Palestinian youth drinks mint tea with his father. Behind them, pictures of Arab singers and film stars share space with typical Palestinian embroidery and a rug depicting Mecca.

Accompanied by his children and some of his sheep, a Bedouin enjoys a glass of tea in his woven goat-hair tent. Most Bedouin tents are divided into two parts: women retire to their own area to cook, or when guests appear.

tourist spot. In the older, crowded Arab part of the town, robed Muslim dignitaries walk silently to prayers through the courtyard of the domed Al-Jazzar mosque with its slender minarets; it sometimes seems that little has changed since the Ottomans ruled.

To the west of Haifa, in the lush vale of Jezreel, some Israeli kibbutzim have established high-technology industrial enterprises. To the regret of the kibbutz movement's traditionalists, hired Arab workers have taken the place of the collectives' own members in the fields.

In the Galilee, beyond Nazareth, a number of Muslim and Druze farming villages lie between Jewish settlements. The ancient villages seem to have grown out of the stony landscape, but the flourishing crops in the fields around them indicate that Arab farmers, like their Jewish neighbours, have begun to reap the benefits of modern farming methods and better equipment. Quietly prosperous, the local Arab population has now outstripped the Jewish population, and Arabs once again, as they did before statehood, form the majority in Galilee.

In the coastal plain between Haifa and Hadera lies the so-called "Arab triangle", a tight nucleus of villages where the farmers, like their counterparts in Galilee, have moved from subsistence farming to the more intensive cultivation of cash crops. The visible signs of this progress often disappoint the tourist photographers, who prefer their Arab villagers in unchanging biblical poses—barefoot *fellahin* painfully dragging ploughs over rocky soil, shepherds with their pipes and goats, women carrying water jars to the well. Nevertheless, the villages in the triangle have prospered and expanded, sharing to some extent the economic

4

growth of Israel as a whole. Farming is no longer the only source of income. Here, as in other parts of the country, Arabs have replaced Jewish workers on building sites and now dominate the construction industry, not only as unskilled labourers but as foremen and prosperous independent contractors.

To find the more exotic Arab of their fantasies, sightseers are compelled to travel farther south into the Negev, home to about 40,000 Bedouin. Yet even these desert nomads are slowly being settled in permanent sites. For some years, the authorities unsuccessfully tried to persuade the Bedouin to move into blocks of modern high-density housing. Eventually realizing that many of them emphatically preferred their traditional tents, the government changed its policy. Now extended-family groups are given vacant plots for development. Some still live in tents, others in shacks, and a few in large villas. Many families have modern houses which they use, in the main, as storerooms, continuing to eat and sleep in tents pitched alongside.

Less interested than other Arabs in the politics of the world outside, Bedouins instead focus their attentions on the weekly market in Beersheba, where, as of old, they haggle energetically over sheep, chickens, herbs, spices and traditional handicrafts, as well as more prosaic manufactured goods. The vendors of intricate Bedouin bracelets and those of bright plastic buckets ply their wares side by side with no sense of incongruity.

The Israeli authorities are eager to note the qualitative improvement in the lives not only of the Bedouin but of all Israeli Arabs since 1948. Before then, few if any Arab villages had running water or electricity; by 1972 the

national electricity grid had reached nearly ever Arab village, with running water in every house. Arabs, like all Israelis, enjoy far better health; life expectancy has increased from 54 in 1948 to over 70 in the 1980s. They are also better educated: by 1984, 95 per cent of Israeli Arab children were enrolled in school, and more than 2,000 Arab students attended Israeli universities, while another 1,000 studied abroad.

But for the Arabs of Israel, an improvement in living conditions is not the only point at issue. There are other, and deeper, forces in the Arab-Jew equation: forces of hatred, fear and pride that have distorted the relationship of the two peoples, despite their

common ancestry and religious roots.

In response to the growth of Zionism at the end of the 19th century, a new nationalist consciousness emerged in Palestine. Many of its first activists came from the small, highly educated élite of wealthy landowning families in Jerusalem (ironically, others of the same group were profitably selling out to Zionist buyers). But political literacy was not solely the preserve of the rich: teachers, shopkeepers and government clerks, who now served the British as they had served the Ottomans before them, were aware of nationalist stirrings elsewhere in the Arab world.

The Zionist settlers and their alien ways troubled this Muslim society. For

centuries, the Arabs of Palestine had tolerated small, impoverished communities of pious Jews who had lived quietly among them, keeping themselves to themselves. But these brash newcomers—with their irreligious socialism, their bare-legged women working in the fields with the men—offended Arab sensibilities.

The turbulence of the years that followed drove the two peoples even further apart. The hope of early Zionists that the Jew and Arab might share the efforts and rewards of building a new Palestine together became an ever-more unlikely fantasy. As Zionist activity increased, Arab militancy grew. When the British appointed the young Arab nationalist Haj Amin El Husseini (member of one of Palestine's largest landowning families) as Mufti of Jerusalem in 1921, the pattern for the next three decades was set.

Universally acknowledged as a "charmer" and a "suave diplomat", the red-bearded Husseini, leading a coalition of Palestinian clan leaders, urban professionals and rising political activists, was implacable in his opposition to Zionism. He refused to accept the Zionist presence in Palestine or to negotiate with them directly on any issue. But while the Arab nationalists declined to yield at all, the Zionists took a more pragmatic course, purchasing a little more land in one place, building a Jewish school or hospital in another, keeping pace with the tide of international opinion and confident of the ultimate triumph of Jewish nationalism.

Ironically, the Mufti gave his support to the Nazi government in Germany, whose persecution of Jews was ultimately the factor that created an international concensus in favour of the Jewish state. Husseini's propaganda

broadcasts during the war, sponsored by the Nazi government, eventually landed him in a French prison on a charge of collaboration.

After the new Jewish state had declared its independence and defeated its Arab opponents in the bloody conflict that followed, the Arabs named the events of 1947–49 "the Great Disaster". By the time the fighting ended, an indeterminate number of Arabs—possibly half a million people—had fled the new state of Israel, leaving behind about 167,000 of their fellows, mostly poor peasants. Some families had managed to leave with most of their possessions before the fighting started, and had resettled

themselves in newly thriving Arab states, such as Kuwait; others found homes farther afield, in Europe or the Americas. But the majority of the Arab refugees were not so fortunate, and spent a wretched winter huddled in Gaza, in Jordan, Syria and Lebanon. It was the Palestine Arabs who were now scattered, in their own Diaspora.

Unwanted by neighbouring Arab nations, the homeless Palestinians, many of them women and children, were gathered into 53 United Nations Relief Works Agency (UNRWA) camps in Jordan, Syria, Lebanon and Gaza (which the Egyptians had annexed at the end of the war). The camps were a breeding ground for a rising

A YOUNG RELIGION WITH A FAITH IN HUMAN UNITY

The Baha'i shrine in Haifa.

Israel is the world centre of the Baha'i faith, inspired by the teachings of Mirza Ali Mohammed, a 19th-century Persian mystic. After he was martyred in 1850, his doctrine was expanded by disciple and compatriot Baha' Allah ("Glory of God"). The religion combines elements of Islam, Christianity and Judaism, and teaches the essential unity of mankind.

Only a handful of the hundreds of thousands of Baha'i adherents live in Israel; the rest are scattered worldwide. But the faith found its base here when Baha' Allah, after years of wandering, ended his days in Palestine. In 1899, seven years after Baha' Allah's death, followers had the exhumed body of Mirza Ali Mohammed brought to Haifa and entombed in a shrine, which was later topped with a golden dome—a gift from believers around the world.

A Pentecostal minister and his helper baptize a swimsuited woman in the River Jordan in Galilee while others wait their turn. Many of Israel's 96,000 Christians and thousands of foreign pilgrims choose to be baptized in the river—as Christ was 2,000 years ago.

nationalist group called the Palestine National Liberation Movement, (later absorbed by the Palestine Liberation Organization). Its members expressed the frustrations of their people, despairing of any help from their host-countries, who had resolutely kept them in their camps. By 1959, one of its leaders, Yasser Arafat, was preaching that the Palestinians should rely only on themselves for the liberation of their country and that their weapons would be terrorism and guerrilla warfare.

At first, life was not much easier for the Arabs who remained in Israel after 1948. Most of the main concentrations of Arab settlement fell within the "security zones" in the border regions, which were under military rule. Here, lands were confiscated, whole villages were razed to the ground and their inhabitants resettled. Villagers wishing to travel outside their own districts needed permits from military authorities, curfews were imposed and communications often suspended. Arabs felt that the government often used "security reasons" to justify their oppression of the non-Jewish population. Not until 1966 were the military restrictions lifted, the application of regulations liberalized, and Arab workers allowed

Bedouin children stand in the opening of a tent pitched outside their house near Beersheba. The government has constructed houses for many of the nomads to encourage them to settle, but this building is mostly used as a storeroom while the family continue to live in their traditional dwelling.

to join the Israeli General Federation of Labour, the Histadrut.

Despite these reforms, many Israeli Arabs still question Israel's claim to accord full equal rights to all its citizens. Though public notices are bilingual, and Islam, like Judaism and Christianity, is a recognized religion, Arabs often feel the victims of discrimination.

Although Arab citizens enjoy the same voting rights as other Israelis, many of them resent the fact that there is no specifically Arab political party. The government, giving the official excuse of "national security", refuses to permit the formation of any political grouping that might espouse the cause of Arab nationalism. Arab towns and villages have their own democratically elected local councils, filled from a slate of Arab candidates, and in general elections Israel's political parties compete hard for Arab votes. Among the 120 members of the Knesset, there are about seven to 10 Arab members, usually from the centrist and left-wing parties. The long-established Communist Party, for example—officially anti-Zionist though not against the state of Israel's existence—has traditionally been a natural magnet for the Arab protest vote.

Despite official Israeli statistics that show continuous Israeli-Arab progress in education, housing, health and purchasing power, the Arabs unsurprisingly compare the quality of their lives with the even higher standards of their Jewish neighbours. The Israeli statistics do not reveal that there are upper limits to Arab progress, but according to a 1984 U.S. State Department report on human rights, fewer than 2 per cent of Israel's senior government officials and 3 per cent of judges were Arabs, although Arabs made up 15 per cent of

the population. No large bank or industrial enterprise was headed by an Arab; and in Israeli universities, 3 per cent of students and an even smaller percentage of the academic staff were Arabs.

The usual Israeli reply to criticisms such as these is that as long as the wider Israeli-Arab conflict continues unabated, it is unlikely that Arabs will be appointed to senior government or civil service posts, except in special cases. Ambitious Arab graduates are faced with few options: the so-called "free professions", such as medicine, law, engineering, teaching or journalism. And even in these fields, Arabs feel there are limits to their advancement.

Discrimination operates, the Arabs say, throughout the economic spectrum. They claim that many Arab farmers, whose lands were confiscated, have been reduced to day-labourers on Jewish co-operative farms and kibbutzim. In industry, Arabs feel they are left with the rump of the low-paid, unskilled jobs, while Jewish workers move into better-paid, high-technology fields and defence-related industries.

Polarization, however, begins long before people enter the work force.

Jewish children automatically go to Hebrew-language state schools, and Arab children go to parallel Arabic-language state schools. Only when they reach higher education do the two groups converge. Even then, many young Arabs resent the fact that they must pass the *Bagrut* examination in Jewish history and literature before they can matriculate. Not surprisingly, Arabs fortunate enough to enter the universities often feel themselves in an alien environment. Their Arab student unions are given official blessing but remain a guarded refuge, where memories of the "Great Disaster" mingle uneasily with frustration, militancy and an unquenchable national pride.

At the University of Haifa, where Arabs make up 10 per cent of the students, a special Arab-Jewish centre has been set up to promote coexistence and "shatter mutually hostile stereotyping". The centre awards scholarships to Arab students and arranges pre-academic courses for them in Hebrew and English. Arab students co-operate in research into Arab life in Israel and the Middle East generally. In Middle East studies, both Jewish and Arab lec-

Carrying the day's bread, a Palestinian woman and her daughter emerge from their centuries-old underground oven. The bread is leavened with fermented dough from a previous baking and cooked on hot stones—a method which goes back at least 12,000 years.

4

turers have been appointed, in an effort to present a balanced picture. Yet even its most enthusiastic supporters accept that a liberal academic island of coexistence in a place like Haifa University will remain just that—an island—so long as the general Israeli-Arab conflict remains unresolved.

Suspicion, contempt or outright dislike between members of different ethnic groups is not unique to Israel, but the unresolved hostilities between the Jewish state and the Arab world do nothing to help the problems of prejudice at home. Many Arabs feel they are victims of ill-feelings that range from mild distrust to sheer bigotry.

Although cases of Israeli Arabs harming their Jewish compatriots are extremely rare, Arabs complain that the Jews can never rid themselves of the notion that the Israeli Arabs constitute a fifth column within their boundaries. In the 1970s, the many incursions by guerrillas of the Palestine Liberation Organization did nothing to alleviate such fears. Between 1977 and 1984, tensions between Arabs and Jews increased even more under the right-wing Likud government. Arabs saw a sharp swing towards a new assertive Jewish nationalism: the Gush Emunim, an extremist group largely composed of North American immigrants, claimed the West Bank to be Jewish by divine right, as part of the biblical land of Israel. In 1985, a group of Jewish terrorists were convicted of the murder of three Palestinian students in the West Bank town of Hebron; other members of the same organization were accused of conspiring to blow up the Dome of the Rock, the sacred Muslim site on the Temple mount in Jerusalem. Not surprisingly, many Israeli Arabs—particularly students—sympathized

Young Arabs walk to their school near Mount Carmel. Education is compulsory for all children in Israel, including those in the occupied areas. Arabs are taught their own language and culture, but after the age of nine they are also obliged to learn Hebrew.

with the anti-Israel views of the PLO.

Yet even in the midst of conflict, some attempts are being made to heal the rifts and smash the myths that engender prejudice. A new "coexistence" course, entitled "The Arab Citizens of Israel" now features on the curriculum of Jewish-Israeli schools, and an equivalent programme has been introduced into the Arab-language system. For many young Jews and Arabs, the course provides a unique opportunity to meet their counterparts face to face; they do not flinch from asking hard questions and telling difficult truths.

"Why," asked a Jewish student, "should I accept someone like you, who gives legitimacy to the PLO? They want to kill me."

"I believe that the PLO is the representative of the Palestinian people. O.K., I am part of the Palestinian people . . . but I see myself as a citizen of Israel, entitled to equal rights."

In the zones occupied by Israel after the Six Day War of 1967, Arabs today still live under military restrictions, as Israeli Arabs did until 1966. Many consider themselves in a political limbo

112

while the international community debates their future. Recent history has placed the Jerusalem Arabs in a particularly difficult position, victims of the intense nationalist and religious passions which both Jew and Arab feel for the city. Yet for the most part the two peoples coexist harmoniously. Ethnic tensions erupt here far less often than they do in other centres with polarized populations; the atmosphere in Jerusalem is infinitely more tranquil than it is, for instance, in Belfast.

The Arab name for Jerusalem is *al-Quds al-Sharif*, which means "the Holy and Noble City". Here, in the seventh century, the Arabs built a mosque, the Dome of the Rock, to mark the spot where Muhammad himself is said to have departed on his journey to heaven. The Jews' attachment to the city is equally powerful, going back nearly 3,000 years. The Psalms praised the ancient capital as a "perfection of beauty"; the prophet Isaiah called it "the faithful city full of justice, in which righteousness lodged".

To Jews the recovery of Jerusalem was a homecoming of deep emotional significance; to Arabs it seemed to set the seal on the humiliation they suffered in the "Great Disaster"; they had their doubts about Isaiah's encomium to Jewish justice and righteousness. When Israel unilaterally annexed the previously Jordanian half of the city and declared Jerusalem the nation's capital, the United Nations refused to recognize the annexation; many foreign governments chose to keep their embassies in the former capital, Tel Aviv. Encouraged by these gestures, many Arabs retained a hope that they might, in the future, become masters of their own destiny in Jerusalem.

In the aftermath of the Six Day War, the task of reuniting the fragmented city fell to its new Jewish mayor, Teddy Kollek. He took it upon himself to oppose what he saw as the bias of the government and their tendency to ignore the needs of Jerusalem's Arabs. He objected to policies that would transform Greater Jerusalem into a purely Jewish capital, guarded by strategically placed Jewish suburbs along the skyline. Jerusalem, he insisted, should be a city with an international flavour, where the Jews and Arabs respected each other as fellow citizens. Through

mortgage companies linked to the municipality, he conjured up thousands of loans for Arabs wanting to build their own homes, and saw to it that Arabs received their share of new school buildings and recreational facilities. Above all, he demanded that Arabs be employed at every level of local government. In return, Arabs turned out in large numbers to vote for Kollek in municipal elections, ignoring PLO calls for them to boycott the polls.

Kollek's pragmatic politics seemed to provide the only solution to the anomalies that confronted the Israelis when they first annexed East Jerusalem. They discovered, for example, that in legal terms Jerusalem's Arabs became Israeli inhabitants while remaining Jordanian citizens; they thus acquired the problematical status of resident enemy aliens. They found it difficult to persuade Arab practitioners of professions, businessmen or company directors to apply for licences under Israeli law, to pay Israeli taxes, or to conform with laws applying to the employment of municipal workers.

Some laws, the Israeli authorities decided, were best left unenforced; the others have been amended to make special provision for the Jerusalem Arabs, who are now entitled—but not compelled—to become Israeli citizens. The Muslim religious courts, which operate in accordance with the Islamic laws of Jordan, have been left intact, and Muslim control over the Temple Mount retained. An attempt to impose an Israeli Arab curriculum in East Jerusalem schools resulted in demonstrations by pupils and teachers, and most Arab parents simply transferred their children to private schools that followed a Jordanian curriculum. The authorities have now quietly dropped

4

In a marble factory on the West Bank, a Palestinian cuts stone for export to Jordan. Israelis point out that since the 1967 occupation the economies of the territories have expanded and unemployment among the Arabs is now little more than one per cent.

the issue, in favour of the *status quo ante*.

For many Jerusalem Arabs, Israeli annexation has made little difference to their way of life: in some respects they are better off economically than they were before. After the Israelis restored and rebuilt parts of the city, tourism increased, and the Arab quarter—chaotic, crowded and noisy—has lost none of its character. Chic Arab-owned boutiques and shops cater for the foreigners thronging the cobbled alleys to haggle for carpets, brassware and antiquities of dubious age. Middle-class Arabs have become more prosperous, and patronize the same international hotels and restaurants as Jews. On Saturdays, when Jewish shops are closed for the Sabbath, long queues of cars bring Jewish customers eager to stock up on provisions at the Arab shops in the Old City, which is now almost exclusively inhabited by the middle classes. Wealthier Arabs have moved into the suburbs of Greater Jerusalem, to live in more spacious surroundings.

Jerusalem has long had a substantial population of Arab professional people; many of the older generation received a European education under the British Mandate. The city is still provided with power by the Arab-run Jerusalem Electricity Company, and serviced by Arab doctors, lawyers and municipal officials working alongside Jewish colleagues. Many members of the Knesset, Jews as well as Arabs, have Arab secretaries. Arab journalists staff the four Arab newspapers published in Jerusalem, and produce the programmes for Israel's Arab radio and the Arabic-language television.

Despite a climate of prosperity and productivity, Jerusalem Arabs are still not reconciled to Israeli annexation. The warp of bitter Arab antagonism to-

wards Zionism is now woven with a weft of fatalistic resignation to the apparent permanence of the Israeli presence. Many Jerusalem Arabs regard the PLO, once their best hope of self-determination, as a spent force. They have seen new Israeli settlements, which were heavily subsidized and encouraged by previous governments, surround the city on former Arab land, and they have watched the Jewish population of Jerusalem rise to become the majority. They feel oppressed by the Israeli censorship of Arab newspapers, which has often been crudely exercised in the name of "security". They draw little comfort from the freedom of expression—which frequently espouses Arab causes—that is enjoyed by the Jewish press, only noting that the official censorship regulations seldom seem to be applied with equal rigour to Hebrew-language newspapers.

An Arab baker in Hebron displays a platter of *baklava*—layered pastry with nuts and honey. In Israel, both Jew and Arab share a passion for these sweetmeats, which are thought to have originated in ancient Persia.

The atmosphere is perceptibly different outside Jerusalem, in the 5,500 square kilometres of the West Bank proper. Although only the fringes of the Arab population actively resisted the Israeli occupation, resentment remains widespread. But the Arabs themselves have yet to agree on a desirable alternative. Some are supporters of the PLO; others are less keen on the domination of what they see as a faction-ridden movement. Older Palestinians have unpleasant memories of 19 years of harsh Jordanian rule between 1949 and 1967, and there is no desire for close links with undemocratic Syria. Faced with such a Hobson's choice, few West Bank Arabs could foresee any prospect of genuinely democratic self-rule that would accommodate peaceful coexistence with their Israeli neighbour.

North of Jerusalem in the West Bank lies Nablus, a quiet town of villas and

small gardens. A centre of Arab nationalism, with a new Jewish settlement on the skyline and an Arab university below, it is the site of a large refugee camp. Nablus is also the home of noted writer Raymonda Tawil, one of a number of Palestinian intellectuals who has kept alight the flame of nationalism. In her book *My Home My Prison* (first published in Tel Aviv), Tawil relates how, in 1967, on the second day of the Six Day War, she and her friends saw a column of tanks trundling down the main street. At first she imagined them to be a unit from a friendly town's Arab army—Algerians, perhaps, or Iraqis—come to help the Palestinians in their hour of need. Then she realized, in

horror, that these were Israeli troops: after barely two days' fighting, they had driven the Jordanians from the West Bank and the Egyptians from the Gaza Strip. This moment, she admits, shattered any illusion that Israel might be defeated, or somehow cease to exist.

Neither Gaza nor the West Bank had been treated well by its previous rulers. Gaza, a small citrus-growing centre and Mediterranean fishing port, had in 1948 been overrun by Palestinian refugees. They were accommodated in UNRWA camps, hastily built townships with monotonous rows of minimal houses. Relief workers doled out adequate food rations and clothing, and provided good schools and medi-

cal services, but there were few other amenities; life in the camps was bearable, but bleak. Yet, apart from receiving a few hundred Gaza students into Egyptian universities, the Egyptian government, who had sovereignty over the area, did little for the Gaza refugees. They were simply kept on site, bored, depressed and resentful.

On the larger, Jordanian-held West Bank, the 1948 refugees formed a much smaller proportion of the Arab population. Indeed, if work had become available they might well have been absorbed into the community. The Jordanian government, however, playing safe, concentrated all its economic development and interest on the opposite

4

side of the Jordan river. Nor was Jordanian rule gentle, as the Palestinian refugees rapidly learnt. Jordan allowed them no freedom of speech, denied them a free press and refused to permit any autonomous political organization. All political parties on the West Bank were abolished; Jordan's military intelligence was active everywhere.

After their stunning Six Day War victory, the Israelis had apparently intended to return the whole of Sinai to Egypt and the Golan Heights to Syria, in exchange for guarantees of peace and demilitarization. They had also hoped to negotiate an agreement over the West Bank with King Hussein of Jordan. But an Arab Summit Conference in Khartoum in September 1967 rejected compromise in what came to be called the "triple no": no peace with Israel, no recognition, no negotiation.

In the ensuing deadlock, the Israelis found themselves with tempting land on their doorstep. First into the territories had been the Israeli military and administrators; now came businessmen seeking trade and employers seeking Arab workers. Later came religious militants of the Gush Emunim.

The Israeli government resolved that the territories had to be pacified. In the Gaza camps the PLO had left guerrillas behind, and Arabs accused of co-operating with Israel were assassinated. The Israelis set themselves to root out active resistance, and succeeded. They did the same on the West Bank where the Jordanians had, in 1967, conveniently left behind intelligence files on West Bank militants.

In September 1970, King Hussein decided that the PLO posed an increasing threat to the security of Jordan and moved to expel them from his country. After a period of heavy fighting, known

afterwards by the PLO as "Black September", Hussein succeeded. Once the threat of guerrilla raids from Jordan was removed, Moshe Dayan—then Israeli Minister of Defence—declared that the bridges across the Jordan should be thrown open. Within a year, an estimated 100,000 Arab visitors came across the bridges to the West Bank and Israel, and West Bank farmers and businessmen traded freely with the Jordanians as well as the Israelis.

The Yom Kippur War of 1973, however, again threw a shadow over the West Bank. In the following year, King Hussein of Jordan, despite his earlier opposition, acknowledged the PLO to be the sole representatives of the Palestinian people; many West Bank residents welcomed the move with enthusiasm. The Israelis tried to counter this Arab nationalist upsurge by stricter rule, exiling two pro-PLO Arab mayors, dismissing others and creating a conservative Arab "Village League" to oppose PLO activity. A tense situation was made worse when extremist Jewish settlers entered the fray as counter-terrorists, badly injuring the mayors of two Arab communities.

The Likud Government of 1977–84 was accused by its opponents of having violated the concept of "local and cultural autonomy" for the Arabs of the West Bank and Gaza enshrined in the 1979 Camp David agreement between Egypt and Israel. Instead, they had effected *de facto* annexation. Israel faced a crucial dilemma: either it could withhold legal Israeli citizenship from the Arabs of the West Bank and Gaza, or it could not. If it chose the first option, Israel would no longer be a true democracy, and, if the second, the Jewish homeland would become a bi-national state with two million Arab citizens.

The government made its choice, by doing nothing. And so, in the 1980s, two phenomena began to transform the West Bank. First, in spite of objections at home and abroad, the settlement of Israelis in what they called Samaria and Judaea was given the highest priority and proceeded apace. Strategic roads were built, mostly by Arab workers, along with residential settlements and industrial townships. Within two or three years subsidized cheap housing had transformed parts of the West Bank into an Israeli commuterland. Ordinary Israelis, interviewed in the press, admitted they no longer quite knew where the West Bank ended and where Israel proper began.

Despite these upheavals Israeli rule has brought material benefits. Statistics show that the people of the West Bank and Gaza have made steady progress in education, enjoy improved hospital facilities and better health, and possess more consumer goods. Over 60,000 Arab workers commute to work in Israeli industries and agriculture in places such as Beersheba and Ashdod, close to the occupied zones.

The other agent of change has been the presence of five Arab university institutions that now serve the West Bank and Gaza, where there had been none before. The presence of 11,000 to 12,000 Arab students has produced a marked social change in the occupied areas. As a new educated class, they have embraced the Palestinian cause. At Bir Zeit University on the West Bank, students have expressed their support for the PLO by strikes, demonstrations, road blocks and occasional stone-throwing at Israeli traffic. The Israelis have responded angrily to these provocations with temporary shut-downs, political censorship and—

when riots have erupted—with shooting.

Although the status of Arabs living in the occupied zones remains unresolved there are signs that tensions may be easing. The government has lifted some of the most galling restrictions on West Bank Arab life. In the United States, a consortium of some of the wealthiest and most influential American Jews and Arabs has established a development bank on the West Bank, and initiated other projects to improve the quality of life for the Palestinians.

Such beginnings may bring hope, but no Israeli government can afford to underestimate the dangers. Within the state's official borders and occupied territories live 3.5 million Jews and two million Arabs. And this Arab population itself embraces a world of differences: between non-citizens and citizens, between Muslims and Christians, between Arab students at Haifa in dialogue with Israeli academics, and Arab students at Bir Zeit University throwing stones in support of the PLO; between Arab journalists smoothly running the Arabic hours on Israeli TV, and Arab journalists on the West Bank daily expressing their dislike of Israel; between the conservative ultra-orthodox Muslims of Hebron, single-minded in their opposition to Judaism, and the more flexible Christian Arabs of Nazareth, voting Communist.

Given these disparate and conflicting elements, what hope is there for co-existence? The answer may belong to Abu Haled, another Arab writer who, like Raymonda Tawil, saw the Israeli tanks rolling into Nablus in 1967. "Do you know what the hardest thing was for me to swallow?" he told Israeli journalist Amos Oz. "That we are two similar peoples, that our fate is interlocked. Am I happy about it? No, not at all. You are not happy about it either . . . You are our destiny. We are your destiny . . . There is nothing we can do about it: here in this land we are welded together, Jews and Arabs, forever."

Inside a hothouse devoted to rose cultivation, an Israeli horticulturist prunes blooms that have become too ripe for export. The country began selling cut flowers abroad in the early 1960s, and by 1982 it was Europe's largest supplier.

SEEKING SELF-SUFFICIENCY

"Israel," observed the nation's first president, Chaim Weizmann, "is the only country where miracles are part of state planning."

In a land whose ancient history is one long chronicle of prodigies and wonders, it is hardly surprising that the economic growth of the modern state should be hailed as miraculous. By any standard, Israel's material progress— the speed of its development over a few strife-torn decades—has been remarkable. In the years since Independence, despite dislocations caused by war, shortages of food and raw materials, and an economy that has sometimes teetered on the brink of collapse, Israel has transformed itself from a struggling, essentially agrarian state into a Westernized, high-technology society.

But the story of Israel's dramatic economic growth, and her equally dramatic economic crises, is less a saga of divine intervention than a tale of human pragmatism amid the hard political facts of 20th-century life. It is also a story that starts generations before its official beginning.

The Jewish community began to lay the foundations for statehood at least 50 years before it had a land. And the nation's founders had a clear idea of what they wanted to create. Reality, however, fell far short of the dream.

Never was a people more ill-equipped to colonize a barren country than the Jewish pioneers who came to Palestine between the 1880s and the 1920s. They were filled with Zionist idealism and mostly with a socialist ideology, and were consumed with a burning desire to rebuild the old homeland of Israel. But they knew virtually nothing of cultivation, or draining malaria-ridden swamps, or creating new industries, and they lacked all the crucial elements of labour, money and know-how. And they knew nothing of the Arabs in Palestine. It all had to be learnt the hard way.

When the first Zionist immigrants arrived in Palestine in the 1880s, they found a poor, pastoral land, a denuded wilderness of sun, sand and salt. It had only one small river, the Jordan, and streams that dried up in summer. There was no coal, no oil. No precious stones or ores sparkled in the rocky hills or marshy valleys of a place lovingly described in the Bible as "flowing with milk and honey".

Some daunted and disillusioned newcomers went home again, unwilling to face the hardships. But others stayed on, determined to change things. The pioneers considered their few assets, decided what they had to do, and set about doing it.

"Our people," wrote one of the early Zionist leaders, A.D. Gordon, "can be rejuvenated only if each one of us re-creates himself through labour and a life close to nature." But to achieve this, the immigrants needed land.

Sympathetic philanthropists, such as the Baron Edmond de Rothschild, provided funds. One of the Baron's early projects—a winery, established in 1882—provided early immigrants with their first industrial enterprise.

In 1901, the Zionist movement set up the Jewish National Fund as "the eternal possession of the Jewish people". To raise money, the Fund placed blue tin collection boxes in Jewish homes throughout the Western world. From the alleys of London's Whitechapel to the slum tenements of New York's Lower East Side, the boxes stood as household symbols of the Jews' longing for a land of their own.

Land bought by the Fund from Arab and absentee Ottoman landowners was leased to prospective farmers, but not sold in perpetuity. In this, the Fund followed the biblical commandment: "The land shall not be sold for ever and the land is Mine." Even today, land acquired from the Israel Land Authority, which controls most of the agricultural property of the modern state, cannot be leased for more than 49 years.

As well as purchasing farmland already in use, the Fund devoted its resources to land reclamation and development. It opened up large areas of wasteland to cultivation: the broad Jezreel Valley, for example, which later became one of Israel's main breadbaskets, as well as the loess-covered wilderness of the Negev, stretching over more than half the state.

The Fund also used its revenues to afforest the mountains of Palestine, stripped bare by centuries of goat and sheep-grazing. When the early settlers arrived, they noted that the country had few birds, presumably because of the scarcity of trees. The call went out to world Jewry to "plant a tree in Palestine", and succeeding generations have had their births, bar mitzvahs and weddings commemorated by pine, cypress,

119

eucalyptus and carob trees set down in the soil of Israel. Since the early 1900s, the Fund has planted over 100 million of these and other species.

The little blue tin boxes of the Jewish National Fund made a significant contribution to these achievements, but the Zionists needed financing on a larger scale to enable more Jews to settle and work in Palestine. At first, the world banking establishment had not looked kindly on the Zionist cause, and the movement concluded that a banking company of its own was the only solution. In 1899, Zionist leader Theodor Herzl wrote in his diary, "The bank is now our greatest concern. Should we succeed, no one will ever imagine what we had to go through; how much courage it took, for in truth we are boycotted by all the large banking concerns."

In 1902, a year after the establishment of the Jewish National Fund, the World Zionist Organization succeeded in establishing the Anglo-Palestine Colonial Trust. By the time of Independence in 1948, it had become established as Palestine's principal financial institution, and was funding new factories, farms and business enterprises started up by Jewish immigrants.

At the outbreak of World War II, these farms and factories became a lynchpin of British defence in the Middle East. Mobilized by the war effort, Palestinian Jews vastly increased the amount of land under cultivation, and built hundreds of new plants, virtually overnight, to supply the Allies with essential military, technical and medical supplies. By 1943, nearly two thirds of the Jewish work force was employed in defence-related occupations. In the short term, this surge of activity aided the struggle against the Axis

powers; in the longer term, it provided fertile soil for the germination of Israel's economy after Independence.

But when the British virtually walked out overnight on May 14, 1948, after 30 years as the ruling power, they left a legacy of administrative chaos that had its economic repercussions.

Reluctant to give any support to the new nation, the British government froze all sterling assets held in Britain by the old government of Palestine, leaving the fledgling state without foreign currency to import food and other essentials. Israel was forced to borrow, in some cases from unconventional sources. The first Finance Minister, Eliezer Kaplan, appealed for loans from American Zionists to buy food.

In spite of the infrastructure of roads, bridges, airfields and harbours that the British had, perforce, left behind them, communications and transportation were beset by difficulties. The International Postal Union at first refused to carry post originating in Israel. Because of exorbitant insurance rates imposed by the British-controlled Shipping Conference, a virtual shipping blockade was imposed.

Rationing had to be instituted. A black market flourished and prices rocketed. As in post-war Europe, the citizens of the new state breakfasted on powdered eggs and drank chicory instead of coffee. Children were allowed two fresh eggs a week. Butter was available, but only on doctor's prescription.

Food was not the only thing in short supply. In 1945 the Arab nations had launched a boycott against Zionist enterprises which, after Independence, became a full-scale economic blockade. They threatened to embargo any company that did business with the Jewish state, and blacklisted those who had in-

vested in Israeli enterprises, joined in partnership with Israeli firms or shipped goods to Israeli ports.

The most serious threat came from the maritime blockade: Israeli shipping was barred from the Suez Canal, as were vessels of other nations carrying cargoes to Israeli ports. In 1949 and 1956, Egypt also blocked the Tiran Straits, the only access to the Israeli port of Eilat.

As a result, Israel could not do business with natural trading partners— its nearest neighbours—and, instead, had to import even the most basic commodities from markets hundreds, even thousands, of kilometres away. Newsprint, for instance, was so hard to come by that newspapers were restricted to two-page editions. To cram in all the news, editors resorted to tiny, hard-to-read type. At the same time, goods produced in Israel for export had to be transported over great distances to find a market, which was hardly a way to keep prices competitive.

But adversity served as a unifying force. Even in the economically precarious years of the late 1940s and early 1950s, public morale remained high. Inspired by its first prime minister, David Ben-Gurion, the new nation set practical goals for itself: to conquer the desert, to build roads, factories and homes, to gather in the exiles. Above all, Israelis had to acquire a new self-image: they were no longer settlers, but owners of an independent state.

The excitement—and the discomforts—of those early years are vividly remembered by Edi Danino, now a prominent trade-union leader, whose family came to Israel from Morocco in 1956, when Edi was 17. "We prayed all our lives to live as free men in a Jewish state," he recalls. But the realities of

Outside a warehouse in the port of Ashdod, a truck driver uncovers a consignment of lemons. Marketed under the "Jaffa" label, citrus fruits account for more than 30 per cent of the country's agricultural exports.

Israel hit hard. On arrival they were taken to a transit camp at Ramla, near Tel Aviv. Not far away was the valley where Joshua had ordered the sun and the moon to stand still. But the biblical associations had little appeal for the family when they saw the accommodation assigned to them. Edi's father took one look at the shack they would have to live in during the oncoming winter and proudly announced, "Not one night will we sleep here." Whereupon he marched out of the camp with his wife, Edi and Edi's sister.

Fortunately, three other sons of the family had preceded them and one had a single-room flat. There the Daninos spent their first months in the country.

Edi remembers how the beds were lined up head-to-foot round the walls of the single room. In the middle was a table and chairs where the family crammed together to eat the meals Edi's mother cooked on a single-burner kerosene stove.

Within three months Edi was called to the army. "That gave the family a little more room. It was tough to adjust, but we were now in our own land and we felt we were building something new for ourselves and our people."

The Danino family, like many of their fellow newcomers to Israel in the 1950s, grumbled about the overcrowding, food shortages and many other inconveniences. But the public shared a

powerful sense of purpose, and conversations that began with a catalogue of complaints usually ended with the words "yi 'hyeh tov"—meaning "one day it will be good". In Edi's case, the improvement was not long in coming. After finishing his army service in 1959 he went to work as a tool mechanic at the large Middle East Pipe plant in Ramla, and became active in the trade union there. Before long he was well on the way to a powerful position as a worker-representative on the plant's board of directors.

The state developed swiftly. From Dan in the north to the new port of Eilat at the southernmost tip, roads, housing, factories and settlements were

5

appearing almost overnight. It was common to hear people say, "I was here two weeks ago, but that building wasn't built then." On a tour of Israel, American television journalist Edward R. Murrow observed that "if the Star of David were not on the flag of Israel, the cement-mixer would be."

Integrating new arrivals was a high priority, but it proved expensive in both money and human resources. The public knew well that even though national growth was clipping along at an unprecedented 10 per cent every year, enormous infusions of capital and time—at least a decade—would be required to achieve Western European living standards. No one expected to grow rich overnight. Indeed it was, and still is, a common Israeli maxim that "if you want to make a small fortune in Israel, come with a large one."

But money was beginning to roll in. About 820 million dollars came in the form of West German war reparations and restitution payments to individual Holocaust victims. Funds came also from the sale of Israel Bonds in the United States and from Jewish contributions throughout the Diaspora.

The growth in the 1950s continued unabated into the next decade; indeed, the early Sixties saw a boom period of rising exports and increasing prosperity. New industries were opening up, while slightly older enterprises began to bear fruit: textiles and leather goods, copper mining, electronics, diamond-cutting and petrochemical production were all rising to profitable heights, and Israelis reaped the benefits of their early hard work and sacrifices.

Even as they celebrated their successes, some Israelis expressed concern about the size of the national debt, and the steady outflow of funds as expen-

sive imports—raw materials as well as consumer goods—continued to exceed export sales. Optimistic economists, however, predicted that, if the current growth rates were maintained, Israel would virtually be able to free itself from its vast balance of payments deficit by the early 1970s.

The Six Day War of 1967 cast a shadow over these rosy prognostications. Defence spending and the production of military equipment took precedence over the manufacture of goods for export, and currency poured out of the country at a prodigious rate, for the purchase of more arms abroad.

The economy recovered rapidly after the war, with full employment, a hefty

increase in tourism—caused in no small part by the desire of foreign Jews to visit a newly reunited Jerusalem and the reclaimed Western Wall—and renewed industrial expansion. Immigration, which had previously been on the wane, suddenly increased, with an influx of newcomers from the prosperous West. But the nation was still spending a massive amount on its defence, and these costs spiralled even higher in the early years of the 1970s, as a consequence of the 1973 Yom Kippur War. At the same time, the nation found itself sharing the economic woes that were plaguing the whole of the Western world; soaring global inflation and the energy crisis served only to compound

A parabolic trough collector focuses sunlight on to heat-absorption pipes containing a fluid capable of reaching temperatures higher than 300°C. Once hot, the fluid is circulated to a boiler and heat exchanger, producing steam which in turn generates electricity.

Covered with netting to minimize surface agitation, a solar pond draws sunlight down through layers of increasingly salty water, heating the brine at the bottom to boiling point. Too heavy with salt to rise, the trapped liquid becomes a heat reservoir, storing energy.

122

the nation's own financial problems.

In spite of an economic situation that grew increasingly unstable in the early years of the 1980s, Israelis who, like Edi Danino, had virtually grown up with the new state could point to signs of solid material progress in every aspect of their daily lives. In the 1950s, for example, Israel had only 31,000 private telephones. By 1984, this figure had increased to 1.6 million. Between 1950 and the mid-1980s, private cars had increased in number by 6,000 per cent; by 1985, they travelled along some 12,000 kilometres of roads, some of them six-lane highways. Sadly, however, the negative side of growth also showed itself on the roads; between 1982 and 1984, for instance, there were nearly three times as many traffic fatalities as there were war deaths in Lebanon during the same period.

Nowhere is Israel's economic progress more conspicuous than in agriculture. Long before statehood, the nation's founders knew that their first priority was to improve the land, to feed both themselves and the waves of immigrants they hoped would follow.

One of the prime movers of these endeavours was a farmer—half Iraqi, half Russian—named Ezra Danin, son of one of the founders of Tel Aviv. Born in 1902, he abandoned a short-lived career as a public official in order to study farming, and dedicated himself to a life on the land. A physically imposing character, tall and heavily built, he was celebrated among his friends for his prodigious appetite for good food, and he was respected among his fellow farmers—Arabs as well as Jews—for his efforts to increase their prosperity.

Danin's farmhouse at Hadera, which was midway between Tel Aviv and Haifa, was a hotbed of agricultural experimentation and innovation. Danin and his colleagues pondered the problem of developing Palestine for the good of all its inhabitants.

Their approach was simple. They had to start by improving the soil. To do this, they needed to find new sources of water, that rarest of raw materials, and they had to learn how to use it as economically as possible. They tried to grow crops that consumed little water—apples, for instance, were rejected as a possibility because the water they used up outweighed the nourishment they provided. Farmers sought to grow currency-earning fruit and vegetables for export, and to produce for themselves those essentials—such as animal feed—that would otherwise have to be imported.

The work could not be done, however, without first educating the people involved—not only the farmers but also the government officials who made and applied the relevant policies. Danin had great faith in farmers, but much less in bureaucrats and planners with their enthusiasm for large, expensive and impractical schemes.

Over a period of 50 years, spanning the British Mandate and the establishment of the state, Danin tackled an extraordinarily wide range of problems in economic husbandry, from experiments with crop species to fish farming.

TAPPING ENERGY FROM THE SUN

Sunshine is one of Israel's few plentiful natural resources, and even before the energy crisis of the 1970s, Israeli scientists were experimenting with ways of harnessing solar power to produce electricity.

Per capita, the Israelis are now the world's largest consumers of solar energy, and the search for new ways to exploit the sun's power continues. Projects now in progress include a pipeline that will carry solar energy over long distances, and a solar cell with a storage capacity that will continue to produce energy after the sun has set.

5

He met with groups of farmers and officials, and convinced them that water and education could help even the smallest farmer to double or treble his crop—and, subsequently, his standard of living.

Danin also provided Israel with one of its most important exports—agricultural expertise. Even at times when foreign relations with many Third World nations were impossible in diplomatic terms, there was hardly a developing African or Asian state that did not seek Israeli help to solve problems which had first been tackled in the farmhouse at Hadera.

What Danin taught and others emulated was a national approach to economic requirements that would also integrate the needs of the individual. He and his colleagues set Israeli agriculture on course with the injunction "Enrich the country, and if you can, enrich also yourselves."

The planning, investment, mechanization and water engineering advocated by Ezra Danin from the 1920s through to the 1970s has paid off. Today the kibbutzim, the moshavim and the smaller number of independent farmers collectively grow more than enough food to feed the population. The nation now earns 10 per cent of its income from agricultural exports.

Farms yield bountiful crops of citrus fruits, avocados, bananas, celery, broc-coli, maize, wheat, pecans, persimmons and flowers. Israeli poultry farmers raise chickens, geese and turkeys, and even ostriches.

Some agricultural innovations have been the result of luck rather than planning, of help by the right people turning up at the right time. In 1952, for instance, a Californian farmer named Sam Hamburg visited Israel for a reunion with long-lost relatives. During his stay he was introduced to David Ben-Gurion. When the Prime Minister discovered that Hamburg was an expert in cotton production, he urged him to come to Israel and start a cotton farm in the Negev. "You grow the cotton, Hamburg, and we'll build the tex-

tile factories," said Ben-Gurion.

The Californian was doubtful. The thin Negev soil was useless for cotton-growing. But when Army Chief of Staff Yigael Yadin took him to the Bet She'an Valley, in the north near the Sea of Galilee, he changed his mind. "We don't have soil this good in California," he announced.

Returning to the United States, he hired a water engineer, then returned to Israel 10 days later. Using conscripted soldiers provided by Yadin as workers, he planted an experimental crop with spectacular results. In little more than a decade, Israel's fully mechanized cotton fields were producing more than its newly built textile mills could handle, and Israel became a cotton exporter.

By the mid-1980s, cotton had become the country's second major crop, outstripped only by citrus fruits. The white bolls now cover more than 54,000 hectares, from the Golan Heights to the northern Negev. Production has been so intensive that Israel, after little more than 30 years of cotton growing, leads the world in yield per hectare.

Most of Israel's cotton is produced by the nation's 270 kibbutzim, which provide 45 per cent of Israel's agricultural products. Following the tradition of improvisation and experimentation handed down by their founders, the kibbutz farms are among the world's most innovative agricultural establishments. Their fish farms, based on artificial ponds with carefully controlled environments, supply record yields of freshwater fish. Kibbutz-produced carp, mullet, and St. Peter's fish, named after the biblical fisherman, provide one quarter of all the fish served on Israeli tables. Many crops are watered by computer-programmed

Seasonal helpers harvest oranges on a moshav—a farming co-operative where villagers own their homes and work individual plots, but market crops collectively. Each moshav houses about 60 families, sharing profits, machinery and responsibilities.

drip irrigation systems, which were pioneered by kibbutz farmers.

High technology has become part of the fabric of kibbutz life. One settlement, for example, faced with the task of providing 3,600 meals daily in its communal dining room, has developed software to programme its menus for a year in advance. Every morning, kibbutz members on kitchen duty receive a printout with all the information they need, including recipes, to prepare and serve the day's food.

On many kibbutzim, high technology has eclipsed farming as a source of income. Today, half of Israel's industrial robots are made in kibbutz workshops, as are many of the solar-energy collectors that heat Israeli homes.

Other kibbutzim have entered the hotel business, to take advantage of the

many foreign visitors that make tourism one of Israel's largest earners. There are kibbutz inns that boast Olympic-sized swimming pools and tournament-standard tennis courts. A luxury hotel on a kibbutz produces some incongruities: holiday-makers, sunbathing in bikinis or sipping gin and tonic on the lawn, may enjoy the sight of others hard at work in boots and overalls, mucking out cowsheds and pitching hay. But, according to Uri Yanai, a bookkeeper at Kibbutz Ein Gev, which serves St. Peter's fish in its Sea of Galilee restaurant and hires out caravans, this does not trouble the kibbutzniks. "The tourists are now competing with the banana crop."

Like the kibbutzim, the moshavim have also extended the range of their activities into manufacturing and retailing. One co-operative, for instance, has supplemented its income by opening a road-side shop selling salamis and art posters.

The changes in the kibbutzim and moshavim reflect developments in the nation as a whole. Few of its people now look to the land for their livelihood. In 1950, 11 per cent of the work force was employed in agriculture. By the mid-1980s, the number had dropped to only 5.4 per cent.

Ninety per cent of all Israeli workers belong to the giant organization officially entitled the General Federation of Labour, but universally known as the Histadrut. Through its manifold industrial, financial, union and welfare activities, the Histadrut is the single most influential force in the Israeli economy. Controlling 43 national, professional and occupational unions, the Histadrut Executive stands behind virtually every wage packet in the nation;

5

the Histadrut's Tel Aviv headquarters are jokingly referred to by Israelis as "the Kremlin".

The Histadrut began in 1920, when 87 workers met in the port city of Haifa to establish an organization that would unite Jewish labour, in preparation for the creation of the Jewish commonwealth. It was a time when thousands of young Eastern European settlers were flocking to Palestine, inspired by the exhortations of the Zionist leader Joseph Trumpeldor, who declared, "I am not tied by anything—I know only one rule: build."

The young radicals formed voluntary labour brigades to construct the roads for a new Jewish homeland. Thirty years later many of these same labourers would take it upon themselves to build a government; Ben-Gurion and other political leaders and trade unionists had all, in their youth, served their time on the road gangs.

Fuelled by the energy of its founders and their grand plans for nation-making, the Histadrut developed into builder and paver, financier and banker, employer and employee, insurer and pension-giver, doctor and nurse. It simultaneously fought for workers' rights and provided seed money and manpower for new enterprises. By becoming owner and controller of the state's major industries, it not only consolidated the power of the Israeli work force, but virtually shaped the economic life of the country. Because its priorities were development and job creation rather than pure profit, it often stepped in where private investors feared to tread.

Cushioned by a staggering array of welfare benefits, the workers of the Histadrut participate on an equal footing with management in the running of this empire. Its diverse enterprises generate 25 per cent of the gross national product, and run the gamut from banking and book publishing to the national bus line, Egged.

The Histadrut's massive construction company, Solel Boneh (meaning Pavers and Builders), accounts for a similar percentage of the country's building activities. During World War II, it built roads and airfields for the British forces throughout the Middle East and Africa, and since that time it has been responsible for domestic projects which range from superhighways to a Roman Catholic basilica. Abroad, its engineers have directed the construction of a NATO airport in Turkey, a bridge in Nepal, dams in Nigeria, a cement plant in Togo, and an entire town hacked out of the jungle in the Ivory Coast.

Another Histadrut enterprise, Koor Industries, is a holding company employing 35,000 workers. Starting out in 1945 as a manufacturer of bricks and baths, Koor played its part in the War of Independence. The Jewish forces, desperately short of defensive weapons and armoured vehicles, asked Koor to armour-plate civilian trucks and buses so they could be used to carry supplies through heavy gunfire to besieged fighters in Jerusalem. Some of them never made it, and their steel bodies, sculpted by artillery fire, still stand at the side of Route 1 between Jerusalem and Tel Aviv. Today, widely diversified, Koor produces everything from pipes to plastics to pilotless planes.

Israel Aircraft Industries, Israel's largest corporation, also developed out of conflict. During the War of Independence, a polio-stricken 30-year-old American named Al Schwimmer, formerly a World War II flight engineer,

A CENTRE OF SCIENTIFIC EXCELLENCE

Lacking the natural resources that have enriched other countries, Israel has sought prosperity by developing advanced science and technology-based industries. It now has the highest percentage of research and development personnel in the world.

Most Israelis involved in this field have been educated at, or work for, the Technion in Haifa, the country's oldest institution of higher learning, founded in 1912. In addition to offering courses to some 6,000 undergraduates, the Technion runs its own research foundation. Projects, funded by the government, industry and foreign sponsors, range from alternative energy sources and genetic engineering to robotics and laser technology. Medical research, stimulated by the needs of Israel's war wounded, is also undertaken.

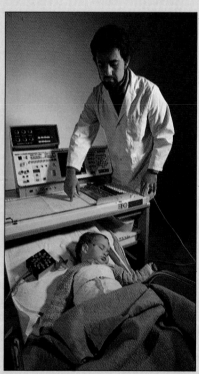

At the Technion Medical School, a sleeping child's recorded brain activity is observed. The school investigates problems such as insomnia or chronic sleepiness, and studies the role of sleep in preventive medicine.

A scientist places a blood sample in a test tube at the Technion's Biomaterials Laboratory; research is being done into the development of artificial blood and plasma that can be stored unrefrigerated. The chief purpose of the project is to improve facilities for casualties in time of war.

A bio-medical engineer fits an artificial arm to a test model. An increase in the number of amputees, caused by the 1973 Yom Kippur War, has spurred the development of advanced artificial limbs, including one type that informs its wearer of movements by means of electronic impulses.

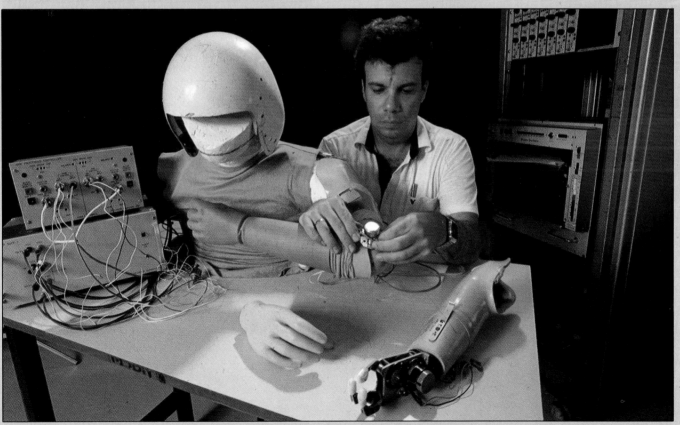

5

scrounged around the world in search of tools and spare parts to build an air arm for the embattled nation. Undeterred by an American embargo on shipments of arms and equipment to the Middle East, Schwimmer gathered together a fleet of used Curtiss C-46 Commandos and Lockheed Constellations at his aviation maintenance workshop in California. He dismantled the planes and crated them to Panama where—so he announced—he was setting up a new commercial airline. Once in Panama, the aircraft were reassembled, and flown to Israel.

Schwimmer's planes provided the starting point for the new Israeli airforce and, later, for the commercial airline El Al. Schwimmer himself, fined heavily by the U.S. government for violating the embargo, moved to Israel and set up an aircraft maintenance plant at Lod, Israel's new international airport. By the 1980s, his company had expanded into an industrial giant, producing state-of-the-art jet fighters and missiles, as well as craft for more pacific purposes, such as executive jets.

Because Israel's weapons systems have been so thoroughly battle-tested, they find ready purchasers worldwide. An early commercial success was the Uzi submachine gun in the 1960s, followed by advanced fighter planes, missile boats, a new type of fire-resistant battle tank and electronic fences to foil clandestine border crossings. By the 1980s, Israel had reportedly become one of the world's major arms exporters, ranked closely behind Italy, the United Kingdom and West Germany. Even nations that do not maintain diplomatic relations with Israel discreetly order its military products.

Much of Israel's high-technology research, however, is directed to more peaceful uses. Israeli scientists have created new products and processes in communications, graphic reproduction, micro-computers, and medical technology. One electronics company, for example, has developed a new diagnostic system known as nuclear imaging. This process produces detailed cross-sectional images of the body and simultaneously measures the average chemical composition of body tissue. The system can pick up changes in tissue chemistry that would not be visible in electronic scans, and it has none of the radiation risks associated with conventional X-rays.

Less dramatic, perhaps, than nuclear imaging, but likely to bring relief to millions, is the rhinotherm, developed at the Weizmann Institute of Science. By delivering concentrated doses of heated air to the nose and the sinuses, the rhinotherm inhibits the growth of the viruses that cause nasal congestion and sneezing. Its advocates describe it as the closest thing yet found to a cure for the common cold.

Nearly 6 per cent of the Israeli work force is employed in these and other high-technology industries; another 30 per cent earn their living in public and community services. But no matter what sector of the economy he or she works in, one of the more perplexing aspects of an Israeli's life is the pay slip,

GIFTS FROM FRIENDS ABROAD

One of the first things that the visitor to Israel notices is the number of plaques commemorating overseas individuals or organizations who have contributed funds or amenities to the state. These inscriptions can be seen on hospitals, ambulances, student hostels, park entrances— even on the back of a chair *(right)* donated for the use of pilgrims at Jerusalem's Western Wall.

Indeed, the financial support of Diaspora Jewry has been crucial to the establishment and economic survival of Israel. By far the largest single source of funds is the United Israel Appeal, to which American Jews alone contributed more than $4 billion between 1948 and 1986.

colloquially known as the "loksh", or noodle, because it is long and thin. These pay slips are only a centimetre wide but sometimes reach a length of 60 centimetres, and are as difficult to disentangle as a mound of spaghetti.

A typical example is the monthly pay slip received by Joseph Neipris, a senior lecturer at the Hebrew University's School of Social Work in Jerusalem. On the income side, there are no fewer than 15 separate items: included among them are basic salary; seniority pay and an advance on a salary increase currently in arbitration; the bus fare to the campus (three minutes away from his home); an allowance for car ownership, plus something called "re-imbursement for car expenses", as well as an advance on a car allowance increase also under negotiation; "erosion" supplements to make up for losses due to inflation on both basic and seniority pay; a telephone allowance; an additional unspecified 4 per cent allowance ("I'm not sure what that's for," admits Neipris); and, finally, three supplements for research expenses representing 5 per cent, 9 per cent and 25 per cent respectively of his basic salary.

The deductions on the pay slip are smaller in number but substantial in size: income tax; National Insurance; Sick Fund; two obligatory provident funds; dues for an academic organization; university life insurance; and funds for advanced study abroad. Once these deductions have been made, Neipris has just over half his salary left to take home.

In compensation, however, he receives the benefits of a wide-ranging social security system that literally covers Israelis from cradle to grave, providing everything from substantial maternity grants to free burial plots. The system also offers generous disability insurance, and pays the salaries of workers released for army reserve duty, which is a considerable drain on the public purse since many members of the work force may be on active service at any one time.

To pay for it all, the Israeli worker carries one of the heaviest tax burdens in the world. On average, half of all personal income returns to the government in the form of tax. Besides taxing earnings, the Treasury slaps on substantial value-added tax on all goods and services. Compulsory car deposits are another source of revenue: when an Israeli buys a car, he must deposit an additional sum with the Treasury—in some years, as much as 40 per cent of the car's purchase price—to be returned to the depositor, without interest, 12 months later.

Because the tax load has always been heavy, it is common practice for employers to offer their workers a glittering array of perks and fringe benefits. Some payroll departments display a considerable amount of ingenuity: one electronics engineer, for instance, says that for many years his company paid him a generous "rent" for the space his private telephone occupied in his home. Many workers receive car allowances even if they do not actually own a car, while others are rewarded

Gem traders do business at the Israel Diamond Exchange at Ramat Gan in Tel Aviv, centre of the country's largest export industry. Among the 1,600 members of the Exchange, multimillion-dollar deals are matters of trust—sealed with a casually uttered *"mazal"*, Hebrew for "luck".

5

with a company car or grants for books and clothing. Professors receive free tuition for their children, electricity workers get free electricity for their homes. Since 1975 most of these benefits have been taxed, but they have become institutionalized as an integral part of the wage structure.

In effect, wage policy is set by the government. As the country's single largest employer—with one third of the nation's work force on its payroll—the state controls the labour market. Once the government agrees to higher pay for one group of workers—teachers, for instance—a ripple effect takes place, with other groups of workers, from physicians to postal clerks, asking for

equal pay rises. The demands then spread to private industry.

In the 1980s, Israeli pay packets, like those of workers throughout the world, were sharply affected by inflation. For many years some cushioning was provided by the system of index-linking: at regular intervals workers received cost-of-living allowances in line with the current inflation rate. However, their outgoings were also index-linked, which of course meant corresponding rises in life insurance premiums, electricity bills and other charges.

In part, Israel's inflation problems could be seen as local effects of a global financial crisis. But they were also symptoms of an overheated economy

that was rapidly heading for a blowout. In addition to record-breaking inflation rates, the beginning of the 1980s saw foreign currency reserves shrinking at an alarming rate, and economic growth coming virtually to a standstill.

Even more worrying was a massive foreign debt. In 1984, for example, every man, woman and child in Israel owed foreign creditors—principally the United States government—over $7,000, the largest per capita debt of any nation in the world.

In a country that was accustomed to full employment, unemployment had begun to rise. Some normally healthy branches of the economy were floundering or failing. The construction

industry was near collapse as the government was forced to cut its building programme. The country's first textile factory was on the verge of bankruptcy. Banks, usually the source of huge profits, were reporting losses. Worse still, the public had lost faith in the Israeli currency—the shekel—and shops were quoting prices in American dollars. After years of apparent prosperity, the nation discovered that affluence was an illusion.

Economists had been warning of impending disaster since the boom years of the 1960s. By 1983, leading economist Haim Ben-Shachar concluded, "This fool's paradise has to end." And end it did. On the farms, as in the factories, in the cities and in the development towns, Israelis asked themselves, "What has gone wrong?"

Since Independence, pressures from within and without had forced Israel to grow at a speed that far outstripped its resources. Year after year the country spent beyond its means to pay. But the nation's leaders had determined that survival demanded the swift build-up of a superior defence establishment, full employment and the rapid integration of an immigrant population. As early as 1949, a Jerusalem newspaper editor had commented, "Melting pot methods take too long. We've got to be a pressure cooker."

By marshalling resources abroad, through the establishment of an organization to sell development bonds, by borrowing heavily from banks and governments, by accepting—with some reluctance—restitution and reparations payments from Germany, and by depriving its citizens of all but their most elementary needs, the pressure cooker built up steam. From 1949 to 1972 the growth rate averaged out at 10 per

cent; meanwhile, real income per capita increased at a rate varying between 4 and 5 per cent.

Ironically, both war and peace have been heavy drains, as well as powerful stimuli, on the economy. The 1973 Yom Kippur War disrupted the economy by involving it in huge defence spending. The 1979 peace treaty with Egypt entailed the construction of new defence lines and air bases. The total cost, directly and indirectly, to Israel as the result of the move from Sinai, has not been revealed. One economist involved in a government study suggests the price may have been "in the billions of dollars", even greater than that of the early 1980s war in Lebanon.

Together with military expenditure, which always accounted for the lion's share of Israel's outgoings, private spending soared in the late Seventies. In 1977, the government led by Menachem Begin liberated the economy, encouraged high consumer spending, allowed Israelis to hold foreign currency and increased the standard of

living far beyond the public's genuine ability to afford it. The value of the shekel was kept artificially high and taxes were reduced on imported goods.

The public went on a frantic shopping spree, encouraged by politicians' assertions that "you never had it so good". Purchase of videos, swimming pools and other luxury items became a national craze. "I bought a video," admits Edi Danino, "because all my neighbours were getting them." During the same period of time he also acquired a freezer, a colour television and a new refrigerator.

He was not alone. One Jerusalem woman admitted to a shop assistant that she was buying a vacuum cleaner even though she had no rugs in her house. "I might as well take advantage," she explained. "One day I may buy rugs, too."

Imported foods were selling in the supermarkets at prices that were much lower than local produce, with devastating effects on Israeli farmers.

In the Negev, the moshavim were in a state of panic. Agricultural cooperatives that had burgeoned in the area were losing their domestic and international customers as their citrus fruits, flowers and tomatoes became less and less competitive on the export market. As their debts mounted, the amount of aid they could expect from a hard-pressed government decreased. In desperation, many farmers uprooted their orange groves. Internal tourism also suffered, as Israelis decided it was cheaper to take their holidays abroad than at home.

Currency flowed out of Israel at an alarming rate, using up foreign currency reserves faster than they could be replaced. At the same time the country went deeper into debt as the Treasury

5

printed mountains of money to pay bills, further weakening the shekel.

The major military build-up, the liberalized economy, and uncontrolled consumption combined with stagnant growth resulted in an inflation rate that hovered around a horrific 1,000 per cent. As the shekel plummeted in value, eroding at a rate of 2 per cent a day, Israelis bought American dollars, put their shekels into dollar-linked savings accounts, or safeguarded their monthly wage packets by investing in high-interest, income tax-free bank accounts for periods of a week or two.

"Every Israeli was to be his own financial consultant," said one young computer technician. "The sort of ordinary worker who used to open his newspaper at the sports pages now goes straight to the financial columns, so he can figure out what he ought to do with his money next."

The loss of confidence in the shekel created a huge "black money" market—dollars on which no taxes were paid—that was estimated to run into the billions. Israelis told stories about friends who were buying dollars by the bushel and stuffing them into their mattresses or under the floor tiles.

Late in 1983 the crisis headed towards catastrophe. The banks began to run out of cash, and the Tel Aviv stock market closed for five days to avert financial disaster. The government took emergency steps to rescue the banks and relieve the crisis of confidence, but the measures were only temporary and the basic problems remained: raging inflation, an unrealistically high standard of living, unalleviated government spending, low foreign currency reserves and an enormous foreign debt.

Economic security became top priority for Israelis as the awful truth hit home. The continuing crisis precipitated early elections in the summer of 1984 and, after long political negotiations, a national coalition government took office. Its prime minister, Shimon Peres, a protégé of David Ben-Gurion, announced, "We will not permit the increase in the standard of living to exceed the increase in production." He enforced stern measures, including a temporary freeze on wages and prices, a ban on a wide range of imports, and plans for a massive reduction in government spending. Israelis girded their loins for a period of austerity. For the first time they faced the prospect of high unemployment.

The resulting shock affected every Israeli. Edi Danino, for instance, found himself, at the end of 1984, spending long nights in meetings with the management of the Middle East Pipe Company, trying to find a formula for rationalizing work to avert dismissals. Inside the once-prosperous plant that made pipes for Israel's oil pipelines and for the National Water Carrier, machinery was strangely silent.

"We have taken one order from the U.S. at a financial loss, just to keep the men at their jobs," said Edi. "At home, my son is now out of the army but can't find work, and I'm afraid he'll move abroad. My salary doesn't stretch to the end of the month any more, and my wife has started work as a check-out assistant in a supermarket to help make ends meet."

There were no simple economic solutions to the nation's problems. Quite apart from the fact that Israel was still not earning as much as it was spending, 26 per cent of its income—the largest single item in the budget—went to repay creditors. In spite of its economic woes, Israel had never yet defaulted on a loan, and for that reason its credit was still good.

The principal lender remains the United States government. Over the years the United States has given Israel at least $30 billion in financial aid, with the understanding that a large proportion of the sum would be spent on U.S.-made goods and armaments. In 1984 American aid amounted to $2.6 billion; $1.2 billion of that was a grant to support the economy. Under normal circumstances, the United States doled out its aid in instalments, but when Israel's reserves dropped precariously at the end of that year, the Americans advanced the entire $1.2 billion in one payment. The Americans also allocated $1.4 billion in military aid, which, for the first time, took the form of a grant rather than a loan.

The effect was salubrious, as Israel reported a steep rise in the Bank of Israel's foreign currency account. Improved balance of payments figures, the wage and price freeze, and government spending cuts all helped to restore some tranquillity to the economic community. But Israelis agreed that a major restructuring of the country's economy was necessary.

Some observers felt that the Israeli economy was far too dependent on the American financial aid, and on the continued good will of the United States Congress. At the opposite end of the spectrum, however, were those economists who felt that, in the continuing struggle between the superpowers, Israel's strategic value to the United States far outweighed the amount of American aid actually received. According to this school of thought, the nation's payments for services rendered should be relative to the financial aid America gives to the NATO countries, which in the early 1980s were together receiving almost 40 times the sum granted to Israel.

Whatever shifts may occur in the tides of superpower politics, Israel's own immediate defence needs remain a continuing strain on the nation's economy. Israel spends approximately $10 billion—nearly 30 per cent of its budget—on defence, in comparison to an estimated $70 billion spent by the Arab states. But its citizens have become profoundly concerned about this continuing drain of human and financial resources and its impact on the nation's economic future. In the strife-torn Middle East, lasting peace and true prosperity seem equally hard to attain.

In the final analysis, Israelis accept that the healing of the economy must come not through copious doses of American aid but from Israel's own energy and ingenuity. The future of the state again depends upon the creativity of its pioneers, although in this generation the fields they labour in are likely to be those of scientific research and new technology.

In this respect, the words of David Ben-Gurion are as germane today as they were when he spoke them, in a 1960 address to his own political party: "We have always been a small people, but this small people has occupied a greater place in world history than nations many times its size. We have enemies as no other nation has, and we have friends as no other nation has. Both of them make it necessary for us to undertake tremendous efforts, not only in security and international relations but also in the sphere of pioneering achievement; in the creation of a model society and the institution of revolutionary changes in the landscape and the economy of the country."

133

HARD-WON WATER TO TRANSFORM A WILDERNESS

One of Israel's highest priorities has been to provide enough food for its expanding population, and this, in turn, has triggered off a massive and costly campaign to reclaim the Negev, the 14,000 square kilometres of sun-baked wilderness that make up 65 per cent of the national land area. The initial prospects were hardly encouraging. With annual rainfall around 200 millimetres in the north and less than 30 millimetres in the south, the Negev seemed more suited to scorpions and sand flies than to fruit growers and farmers.

The turning point in the reclamation effort came in 1964 with the completion of the Israeli National Water Carrier, an elaborate system of pipes, conduits and tunnels which was designed to carry water from the Sea of Galilee, in the far north, to the rain-starved areas of the centre and the south. For the Negev itself, the scheme meant an additional 320 million cubic metres of water a year—a 75 per cent increase that gave new significance to the words of the Prophet Ezekiel, who spoke of a time when the desert would be traversed by a great river and claimed that "everything shall live whither the river cometh". By 1985, some 60,000 hectares were under cultivation and a one-time wasteland of sand and rock was yielding its own rich crop of fruit, vegetables, cereals and cotton.

Another vital element in the "greening" of the Negev has been the widespread use of new technology, especially drip irrigation, which cuts out moisture loss by feeding controlled amounts of water direct to plant roots. But the key to long-term development lies deep below the desert itself, where vast deposits of water from the Ice Age lie buried. A small part of this underground reservoir has already been tapped, and like Ezekiel before them, Israeli scientists foresee a future in which the whole great Negev will flow with life-giving water.

A Negev farmer catches water pumped from an aquifer—one of the underground reservoirs helping to transform the desert environment. Although such water is too salty for drinking, it provides moisture for a large variety of salt-resistant crops, from cotton to cucumbers.

Two researchers use a neutron scatter device to emit high-speed neutrons into the parched soil of the Negev. Any neutrons that come into contact with hydrogen—a main constituent of water—show up on the screen, giving a measure of the soil moisture content.

Broad-leaved agave and spicy yucca plants—the former yield an intoxicating spirit, the latter serve as a shampoo base—are watered through hoses by drop irrigation. Developed in Israel in the 1960s, this technique is twice as economical in its use of water as the traditional sprinkler method.

Protected by wire netting against stray
sheep, a pumping station and a
fertilizer tank make their own
contribution to the "greening" of the
Negev. The pumping station is linked
to the National Water Carrier and
provides irrigation for the
surrounding settlements.

A farmer places plastic sheeting over a field of melons to prevent moisture evaporation. Like the adjoining greenhouses, the field is heated and irrigated by pipes fed from the warm water of underground aquifers—this system ensures a constant soil temperature throughout the year.

An Arava Valley kibbutznik controls the irrigation of fields by computer, programmed to operate drip and sprinkler lines according to a pre-set sequence which uses the available water with maximum efficiency. Such technology is playing a major part in the reclamation of the Negev.

Transformed by several days of intensive irrigation, a stretch of desert below the ruined Canaanite city of Arad is carpeted with burgeoning alfalfa. Drought remains a constant enemy, however, and any crops without adequate water would soon be swallowed by the encroaching sands.

BALANCING LAWS OF GOD AND MAN

Its Declaration of Independence guarantees freedom of religion to all inhabitants, but in the eyes of the world and the minds of most of its own citizens Israel is inescapably a Jewish state. In the simplest sense, the state is Jewish because 83 per cent of its citizens are Jews; it exists in its present form partly because of the Zionist movement's efforts to establish a Jewish homeland in Palestine. But the nation's founders wanted Israel to be more than a place of refuge: they hoped that the new state would encourage and exemplify Jewish values of social justice and morality.

Human frailty notwithstanding, these aspirations might be easier to achieve if there was a consensus on what "Jewish values" actually implied. But there is more than one Jewish world view: Jews, in Israel as elsewhere, run the gamut from the pious believers, who adhere scrupulously to every syllable in the ancient canons of religious law, to atheists who identify themselves as Jewish solely on the grounds of their ethnic origins.

Over the past two thousand years, most of the Jews in the world remained faithful to the body of traditional laws and customs—the *halacha*—and those who continue to do so are now known as Orthodox Jews. But since the 1800s many Jews in the West have broken away to develop new approaches, and Judaism now has other branches: Reform Judaism seeks to adapt the religion to modern life, rejecting such traditional practices as the separation of the sexes in the synagogue and the strict observance of the Sabbath as day of rest. Conservatism, a more recent and largely American development, places itself in the middle ground, between the radicals of the Reform movement and the Orthodox. All three strands of Judaism are completely autonomous, with their own theological seminaries and religious congregations. While the two newer groups have a growing number of adherents in Israel, Orthodoxy remains the only form of Judaism officially recognized, with total control of Israel's powerful religious establishment.

Yet not even the Orthodox meet the exacting standards of piety and ritual purity that are demanded by the ultra-Orthodox Haredim, who live mainly in Jerusalem's Mea Shearim quarter and in Bnei Brak, a township near Tel Aviv. The Haredim themselves are divided into several groups, although their lifestyles and clothes are superficially similar—women wear modest, long-sleeved dresses, with wigs or scarves concealing their shaven heads, men wear long black overcoats and wide-brimmed velour hats on weekdays, or knee-breeches, fur-trimmed headgear and silk caftans on the Sabbath.

The most numerous are the Hasidim, who follow the teachings of the Baal Shem Tov, an 18th-century rebel against the excessive pedantry which then dominated Judaism. His empha-

Behind a Hebrew banner in a Beersheba square, a behatted member of the Lubavitch movement winds the leather straps of *tefillin*—a small box of sacred texts, worn during prayer—round the arm of a passer-by. The Lubavitchers strive to persuade non-observant Jews to return to religion.

6

sis on serving the Lord with gladness attracted a mass following. The movement flourished and grew in Eastern Europe and was carried far beyond its boundaries by emigrants. Hasidim traditionally stress deeds over Talmudic erudition, and they give their allegiance to one of several dynasties of *rebbes*, or saintly men, who are venerated as healers and miracle workers.

Fewer in number, but more powerful, are the Mitnagdim. Hard-line guardians of Jewish law, these devotees transferred to Israel the names and traditions of the great yeshivot (religious academies) of eastern Europe, destroyed by the Nazis.

The third major ultra-Orthodox group is the Yerushalmim, comprised of families who have been in Jerusalem since the early 19th century, and who formed the main element of Palestinian Jewry before the arrival of the Zionists. Part of this community, living in Mea Shearim, calls itself Natorei Karta (Guardians of the Gate); its members are militantly anti-Zionist, regarding the secular state as an abomination.

The Natorei Karta use Yiddish, not Hebrew, as their vernacular; they refuse to profane and debase the holy tongue by using it for anything other than prayer. They do not vote or take part in political life, and they will not co-operate with any state institution. From time to time they have even protested to the United Nations over such domestic issues as mixed-sex bathing in Jerusalem swimming pools, the performance of autopsies—which they see as a violation of religious law—and the desecration of ancient Jewish burial places by archaeologists.

Despite the Guardians' extreme resistance to the present state, Jewish nationalism and the Jewish religion are,

for most Israelis, inextricably intertwined. The relationship between them has always created intense debate and controversy, even in the 19th century when the revival of Jewish statehood was no more than a dream. For religious Jews, only the coming of the Messiah would restore them to their ancestral homeland, and any attempt to speed up the process by human intervention was regarded as blasphemy.

For the Zionists, however, the only solution to the so-called Jewish problem—discrimination, persecution and oppression—was to pre-empt the Messiah's coming and set up a Jewish state as quickly as possible. But what kind of state? The founder of political Zionism, Theodor Herzl, asked in his trailblazing pamphlet *Der Judenstaat* (The Jewish State): "Shall we end up having a theocracy?" Herzl answered his own question with a firm negative, declaring that "we shall keep our rabbis within their synagogues, just as we shall keep our armies inside their barracks."

Such a view did little to encourage religious support, and the new movement, led by Westernized, irreligious and often socialist Jews, was shunned by most traditionalists. But the more moderate of them moved closer after the Second Zionist Congress of 1898, which resolved that "Zionism will not undertake to do anything contrary to the injunctions of the Jewish religion". A religious party called *Mizrachi*—an abbreviation of two Hebrew words meaning spiritual centre—was formed; after statehood it would become the National Religious Party (NRP).

Nevertheless, leadership of the Zionist movement remained with the non-religious socialists. When the state of Israel was proclaimed, there was no doubt that the spirit of Theodor Herzl

still inspired his successors. The state was not to be a theocracy. Its Declaration of Independence affirmed that it "would be based on freedom, justice and peace as envisaged by the prophets of Israel", and would guarantee freedom of religion. How emphatically secular the state intended to be was made clear when the religious representatives on the drafting committee failed, after much argument, to win majority support for their attempt to include a reference to God in the document.

It was a portent of things to come that the very birth of the state should be accompanied by this dispute over a religious issue. Since then, the life of Israel has rarely been free of religious controversies. Occasionally these have led to political crises. The state may be officially secular, but its multiparty electoral system makes it possible for minority parties—especially the religious groupings—to wield power out of all proportion to the number of votes they actually receive.

A general election must be held in Israel at least every four years, and Article 4 of the Knesset Law of 1958 provides that this body shall be elected "by general, national, direct, equal, secret and proportional elections". The whole of Israel is one constituency and the electors vote not for individuals but for a list of candidates presented by each party. The total number of votes cast is divided by 120 (the number of parliamentary seats), giving a figure which is the price, as it were, for each elected candidate. In the 1984 election, for example, the number of votes required to elect one member of the Knesset was 20,733.

This system offers generous possibilities for small parties. In any type of election based on a number of constituencies with a "first-past-the-post" winner, small parties might never gain enough support in any one constituency to succeed. They have a much better chance of collecting enough votes throughout the whole country to win one or two seats. In the 1984 election, for instance, no fewer than 13 small parties received sufficient votes to send between one and five of their candidates to the Knesset, to join the representations of the two major groupings, the right-wing Likud and the left-wing Labour Alignment. These two bodies are themselves alliances of formerly separate political parties.

Throughout the history of the state, such fragmentation has meant that no single party has won enough seats to ensure it an absolute parliamentary majority. The party with the largest number of Knesset members has to negotiate with some of the smaller

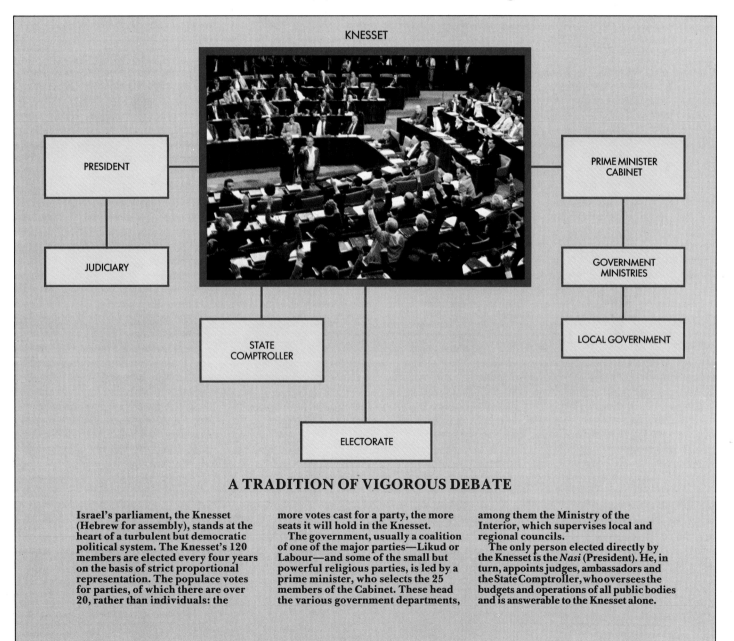

A TRADITION OF VIGOROUS DEBATE

Israel's parliament, the Knesset (Hebrew for assembly), stands at the heart of a turbulent but democratic political system. The Knesset's 120 members are elected every four years on the basis of strict proportional representation. The populace votes for parties, of which there are over 20, rather than individuals: the more votes cast for a party, the more seats it will hold in the Knesset.

The government, usually a coalition of one of the major parties—Likud or Labour—and some of the small but powerful religious parties, is led by a prime minister, who selects the 25 members of the Cabinet. These head the various government departments, among them the Ministry of the Interior, which supervises local and regional councils.

The only person elected directly by the Knesset is the *Nasi* (President). He, in turn, appoints judges, ambassadors and the State Comptroller, who oversees the budgets and operations of all public bodies and is answerable to the Knesset alone.

parties to form a coalition government. Those parties not included in the coalition collectively form the parliamentary Opposition. In the first eight Israeli elections, the Labour Alignment won the most seats and set up the coalitions. The results of the ninth and tenth, in 1977 and 1981, made the right-wing Likud grouping, headed by Menachem Begin, the dominant party.

The 1984 election, however, produced a change in the pattern. Again, neither the Labour Alignment, with 44 seats, nor the Likud, with 41 seats, could hope to form a government on its own. With the country facing the worst economic crisis in its history and with Israeli forces at that time still embroiled in Lebanon, the two rival groups came together to form a government of national unity. (The only other coalition of this kind was formed during the Six Day War of 1967.)

After each election, then, the business of coalition-forming begins. The leaders of the small parties present their terms and begin to haggle: what favours will you do for us if we join you, and help you form a government? In the view of the large parties, the religious parties have always been the most satisfactory of junior allies: not being primarily concerned with the secular fields of foreign affairs, defence and the economy, they have usually been willing to give the coalition leader a virtually free hand on these issues in return for government support for their special religious interests.

Israel has no formal, comprehensive constitution. It was decided, in the first years of the state, that the essential elements of a constitution should be formulated as a series of Basic Laws, enacted separately, that would eventually provide the constitution for the state.

These Basic Laws cover such areas as the role of the president, the function of the Knesset, the machinery of government and the definition of Israel's lands. The Knesset as a whole votes on these and all other major and minor statutes, as well as approving the policies put forward by the Cabinet.

Cabinet ministers—members of the Knesset drawn from the coalition parties—take responsibility for particular policy portfolios and government ministries. Two ministries, those of Religious Affairs and the Interior, are the traditional preserve of the religious parties: they are run by party members, who make sure that the key posts are filled by like-minded colleagues. Through the Ministry of Religious Affairs, the National Religious Party is able to exercise control of the religious establishments and administers a rich source of patronage in the distribution of funds to religious institutions.

The Ministry of the Interior is similarly able to make grants which benefit religious activities. It also provides the link between central government and local authorities: the municipal councils that run the cities and large towns, and the local and regional councils that run villages and rural areas. These bodies are governed by democratically elected councillors, who look after the essential services for their communities: schools, health and social services, road maintenance, sewerage, water supply and other facilities, which are funded by a combination of local taxes and government grants. The Ministry of the Interior exercises control over council budgets, and also supervises their overall administration. More important from the Orthodox point of view, this Ministry also controls matters of nationality, religion and

6

marital status, covering all Israeli citizens alike, whether Jews or non-Jews.

By virtue of their bargaining power in the Knesset and their control over the relevant ministries, the religious parties have secured government backing for legislation to enforce religious observances, and have successfully opposed the introduction of civil marriage and divorce. They have ensured the continuation of a separate religious educational system, and have also maintained the monopoly of Orthodoxy as the only officially recognized form of Judaism. Reform and Conservative Jews, mainly immigrants from the West, have repeatedly pressed for recognition of their movements by the Ministry of Religious Affairs, and, just as frequently, been refused it. The Ministry frequently offered to give these groups the status of a separate religion, placing them in the category of Christianity or Islam. Their proposals were firmly rejected by the indignant representatives of both movements.

Although it maintains departments run by Muslims and Christians to serve the non-Jewish communities and provide support for their ritual needs and religious institutions, most of the Ministry's activities are concerned with Jewish affairs. It controls Jewish life via three establishments: the ecclesiastical courts, the system of local religious councils and the rabbinate, headed by two Chief Rabbis—one serving the Ashkenazi communities, one the Sephardi. Separate but equal, these two supreme officeholders do not always agree; clashes in the 1970s between the Ashkenazi and Sephardi Chief Rabbis approximated the pace and intensity of a world-championship tennis match as each contradicted the other's dictates on points of religious law, ranging from the text of a new prayer book to the morality of Jews living in the occupied territories.

Whichever Chief Rabbi they follow, the Orthodox affirm that Jewish law—the *halacha*—should be the law of Israel. The non-Orthodox, and indeed the non-Jewish minority in the electorate, are bound to disagree.

No Israeli would deny that the power of the religious minority is, in the main, due to its political clout. But to some extent this power also depends on common consent. It is now accepted as axiomatic among the non-religious majority that it was the Jewish religion which preserved the integrity of the Jewish people during the centuries of dispersion. In consequence, the public is inclined to feel that religious susceptibilities should be respected, although, on occasion, there have been angry denunciations of "coercion".

Some of the fiercest controversies between religious and non-religious Israelis arise over the application of ancient religious law to people's private lives. One incident that aroused considerable wrath among the non-observant, and much embarrassment among the pious, was the case of the *Mamzerim* (the Bastards) in 1971. A brother and sister, both serving in the Israeli Defence Forces, became engaged to Israeli Jews. Their mother had been married in Poland to a Jewish convert, but had left him and emigrated to Israel with another man. It was only after she bore her new partner a son and a daughter that she obtained a divorce from her first husband, and married the children's father.

When the children applied to the rabbinical courts for marriage licences, they were refused. According to religious law, children born to a married woman and a man other than her husband are illegitimate and only permitted to marry other such illegitimates or converts to the Jewish faith. The decision outraged public opinion and stimulated demands that civil marriage should be introduced in Israel.

The controversy raged for about a year until it was defused by the application of subtle rabbinical casuistry, which ruled that, since the first husband's conversion to Judaism was doubtful, the Polish marriage was invalid. The two young couples were allowed to wed, and the Chief Rabbi himself performed the ceremony. But the law was not changed. Because Orthodox Jewish rabbis will not solemnize marriages between Jews and non-Jews, those who want to wed outside the faith have to leave the country to do so; however, their foreign marriage is accepted by the state as legally valid, and their children considered legitimate. Divorce, too, remains in the hands of the rabbis, priests and Islamic divines: only the rabbinical courts can grant divorces to Jews, only the Islamic religious courts to Muslims.

When the clerics prove intransigent, aggrieved individuals turn to the Supreme Court. A bizarre case which came before the Court in 1984 concerned the burial of Tereza Anghelovici, a Christian who had come to Israel from Romania with her Jewish husband 20 years before. She lived her life as a loyal citizen of Israel, brought up her children as Jews and, when she died, was interred in a Jewish cemetery. Some time after her burial, the local senior rabbi was made aware of her origins and decided that since the deceased was not Jewish she had no right to lie in a Jewish burial ground. He insisted that her body should be ex-

Demonstrators outside the Prime Minister's Jerusalem residence protest the massacre in Beirut of some 800 Palestinian refugees by Lebanese Christian militiamen. The 1982 Israeli invasion of Lebanon provoked greater domestic opposition than any other war in Israel's history.

humed and interred elsewhere. The Ministry of Health disagreed and, while the argument proceeded, some ultra-Orthodox Jews dug up and removed the dead woman's remains. The Supreme Court ruled that the body be returned to the original Jewish grave.

Even a seemingly uncontroversial subject, such as Daylight Savings Time, raises hackles throughout the community. The economic, energy-saving advantages of advancing clocks in summertime are so substantial that the system has been adopted throughout the Western world. When it was introduced into Israel on an experimental basis in the summer of 1984, however, Orthodox Jews protested that it would encourage Israelis to desecrate the Sabbath: buses and films might start before sunset. One rabbi declared: "What are a few million—or even a few billion—dollars saved on energy compared to what we are losing in spiritual terms?" But cost-cutting on this scale was not dismissed so lightly by the government, and the scheme was formally adopted in 1985.

Yet rabbinical disputations and the scrupulous observance of religious law are worlds away from the concerns of many of the ordinary citizens. "When we lived in the United States," admitted a young Israeli couple who had spent three years in the United States, studying in California, "we went to synagogue every Friday night as a way of identifying with the Jewish community. But here at home, we don't find a need for it. We are Israelis first, and we are part of a Jewish heritage. We know our Bible—it is our history and our culture. But we don't observe religious practices because we don't see them fitting in with modern life." Such views are typical of many members of Israel's younger generation, especially those who have lived or travelled in the West.

The synagogue may be the centre of Jewish community life in the Diaspora, but in Israel it is little more than a place for worship. Architecturally, too, Israeli synagogues are undistinguished: theirs is not a tradition of imposing façades and soaring spires. Most are small, simple and intimate houses of prayer. Jerusalem alone has some 800 synagogues and most cater for tiny close-knit congregations from the same place of origin.

At sunset on Friday evening and early on Saturday morning they are all operating at full strength, particularly in Mea Shearim and in the Old City. Humble rooms are crammed with worshippers, the Hasidim resplendent in their fur-trimmed hats and silk caftans. From street to narrow street in the Jewish Quarter of the Old City, the followers of dozens of different *rebbes* rend the air as they call upon their Maker. Elsewhere, Jews from Yemen, Iraq, Iran, Egypt, India and Ethiopia worship, each with distinctive liturgies, melodies and rituals evolved over centuries in their scattered communities.

Nowhere is the climate of traditional religious life in the Diaspora more carefully preserved than in the 500 state-subsidized yeshivot, the religious academies. Yeshiva students, numbering some 50,000, are exempt from service in the Israeli Defence Forces on the grounds that they are engaged in the spiritual rebuilding of Judaism after the ravages of the Holocaust. They claim that this function is no less vital to the future of Israel than the physical defence of the state. Some of these scholars will become rabbis, but, after many years of study, most will live out their lives within the staunchly observant ultra-Orthodox communities,

6

earning their keep by other means.

Within the milieu known to its denizens as the "yeshiva world", there has arisen a new, post-Six Day War phenomenon: the Yeshivot for Penitents. Within these institutions, Jews from secular, non-observant backgrounds strive to return to the orthodoxy of their ancestors. The schools offer short courses for young Jews coming from the Western world in search of Jewish inspiration, as well as a new way of life for those who choose to stay longer. The first yeshiva of this type was founded by an American rabbi in 1967, at a time when many young American Jews were, like their non-Jewish contemporaries, protesting against the Vietnam War and rebelling against their affluent upbringing. For the generation who back-packed to remote parts to "find themselves", the idea of living in a yeshiva in Jerusalem was as exotic as sitting at the feet of an Indian guru in Benares. To the surprise of some, the Penitents movement, although still small, survived the Sixties and continues to grow. But whether its students are the scions of old Hasidic families or drop-outs from American suburbia, yeshiva education caters for a minority within a minority.

For the bulk of the Israeli population, the source of Jewish education is the national school system. Parents can choose between three forms of education: secular state schools, state religious schools and the ultra-Orthodox Agudat Israel schools, which are outside the state system but receive some funding from the government. Some 70 per cent of Jewish pupils attend the ordinary schools, 25 per cent the state-run religious system and 5 per cent the Agudat Israel institutions. Arab children are educated in a separate state-run system, study Arabic as the main language and receive instruction in Arabic history and culture.

All the non-Arab schools in the state system include tuition in the values of Jewish culture. But while the secular schools use biblical studies as a foundation for teaching history and archaeology, the religious schools concentrate more heavily on religious law and ritual, devoting correspondingly less time to mathematics, sciences and other secular studies.

Judaism, as the religious educational system emphasizes, is a way of life; so all-encompassing is the faith that the Hebrew language originally had no word for religion in the sense of a system of beliefs. Pious Jews follow an elaborately mapped-out sequence of daily rituals. Birth, coming-of-age, marriage and death all have their prescribed customs and ceremonies, and even those who are not otherwise particularly observant will celebrate their weddings under the traditional canopy—marking the exchange of vows by smashing a glass—and later will have their infant sons ritually circumcized in accordance with ancient Jewish law.

But no other event in Jewish life is so important as the weekly day of rest. The fourth of the Ten Commandments enjoins the Jewish people to remember the Sabbath day and keep it holy. "Six days shalt thou labour and do all thy work, but the seventh day is the Sabbath of the Lord thy God." Modern Israel works a frenetic six-day week, but on the seventh day the nation rests and an almost palpable peace prevails.

The holiday runs from sunset on Friday to Saturday evening, ending when the first stars can be seen in the sky. In preparation, nearly all of the Jewish

An elderly man wearing an elaborate silver-threaded *tallith*, or prayer shawl, blows on the *shofar*—a ram's horn fitted with a reed. One of the oldest instruments known to man, the *shofar* is blown on High Holy Days.

THE FESTIVAL YEAR

Many festivals and holy days in the Jewish calendar are observed in Israel as both religious and public holidays. They vary in mood from the solemn days of Rosh Hashanah (New Year) and Yom Kippur (the Day of Atonement) to the happy gift-giving feast of Hanukkah.

One of the most joyous of the festivals is Sukkot *(right)* which occurs over five days during September or October. The holiday takes its name from the makeshift booths that sheltered the ancient Israelites during their 40-year sojourn in the wilderness following the Exodus from Egypt.

Families mark the feast at home by building huts—topped with branches and decorated with fruits and flowers. Other Israelis go on pilgrimage to Jerusalem to visit the giant community *sukkah* on Mount Zion and pray at the Western Wall.

During Sukkot, a dense crowd of men—many with their heads totally covered by prayer shawls—pray before the Western Wall in Jerusalem. Following a biblical injunction, all the men carry a palm branch (the *lulav*), a sprig of myrtle, a spray of willow and an *etrog*—an ancient species of citrus.

Three potential purchasers admire an outsize *etrog*. The fruit, which is grown and bought solely for its ritual rather than edible value, symbolizes the agricultural aspects of the festival, which is celebrated worldwide at the season of the harvest in ancient Palestine.

151

6

Amid the stony fields of the West Bank, south of Bethlehem, an Arab couple guide their mules past new homes for Jewish settlers. For some Israelis, moving to the West Bank is a symbolic act—a recovery of the biblical lands of Samaria and Judaea; others vigorously oppose the settlement.

shops and markets close soon after noon on Friday. So does public transport (although not the privately owned shared taxis known as *sheruts*). The degrees of official Sabbath observance vary: in predominantly secular Haifa, buses continue to run, while in districts with substantial concentrations of Orthodox Jews, the period is marked more rigidly: chains block off streets to traffic and shop windows are dark. But everywhere, even in urban, cosmopolitan and sophisticated Tel Aviv, the hustle of the working week gives way to relaxation and tranquillity. In city, village and kibbutz, the Jews of Israel—observant and irreligious alike—greet each other with "Shabbat Shalom"—a peaceful Sabbath.

But the peace is sometimes broken by those who claim to cherish the divinely ordained day of rest the most. From time to time the serenity of the Sabbath is fractured as ultra-Orthodox Jews, the Haredim, demonstrate angrily and sometimes violently at the desecration of that sacred period by their less religious compatriots. In Jerusalem in such areas as Mea Shearim, the time-honoured rites of Sabbath observance—prayers in synagogues, ceremonial family meals, the recitation of blessings—are carried out in conjunction with a more contemporary ritual: mass-attacks on those citizens who choose to spend their Saturday in secular pursuits. Ear-locked and caftanned residents, young and old, will gather on the roads that skirt their neighbourhood to throw stones at the passing cars that disturb their Sabbath isolation. In the town of Petah Tikvah, a few kilometres from Tel Aviv, near-riots took place every Friday evening for several weeks as Haredim in large numbers held demonstrations against

the opening of the new local cinema.

In addition to the Sabbath, the calendar is punctuated by religious holidays, each with its rich accretion of symbolic acts and ceremonies. The year begins with the High Holy Days—the New Year festival of Rosh Hashanah and the solemn Day of Atonement, Yom Kippur, when the devout ask forgiveness for their sins. These are followed by various major and minor festivals, such as Hanukkah—the midwinter Festival of Lights, commemorating the struggles of ancient Jewish patriots against Roman oppression—and Shavuot, in the late spring, which celebrates the revelation of the Holy Scriptures to Moses on Mount Sinai.

In Israel, non-religious Jews also observe some of these ancient festivals and anniversaries, though not necessarily in the traditional forms. This is particularly evident in the kibbutzim.

The earliest kibbutz members—all good socialists—rejected everything to do with religion. While the secular kibbutzim remain in the majority, some collectives were founded by observant Jews. The leaders of the movement, however opposed to religious rituals, nevertheless recognized that their history was Jewish history, that their holidays were the Jewish holy days and that Saturday was their Sabbath.

As a result, they tried to infuse all the old institutions with new content. In most kibbutzim today, the Sabbath is not merely a respite from work but a day devoted to the refreshment of the spirit, with concerts, plays, lectures, discussions. On the festival of Passover, when Jewish families participate in a Seder—a ritual meal to commemorate the Hebrews' exodus from Egypt and their release from slavery—the extended family of the kibbutz also

holds its own communal feast. In place of the texts that are traditionally read as part of the Seder service, they have created new readings that relate biblical struggles for freedom to more recent events. In all of these, the Nazi Holocaust figures prominently, as does the oppression of the Soviet Jews.

Throughout the Jewish world the autumn harvest festival of Sukkot, or Tabernacles, is observed with synagogue services. But in most kibbutzim it is celebrated in the open air, with pageants, entertainments and displays of the community's own freshly harvested produce and newest manufactured goods: piles of oranges and avocados share pride of place with microchips.

Even in the cities, new expressions have been given to religious occasions. Thousands of Israelis have revived the ancient practice of a Sukkot pilgrimage to Jerusalem; others enjoy a much younger tradition—a wine-tasting festival, celebrating the new vintage from Israel's oldest vineyards, founded by Baron Edmond de Rothschild in 1882.

Purim, commemorating the salvation of the Jews in Persia when the wiles of Queen Esther thwarted a wicked minister's designs against them, has always been one of the most joyous days of the Jewish calendar, celebrated by the reading of the Book of Esther in synagogue and a party for the children at home. In Israel today, it is a national festival, a time of carnivals, costume parades and public entertainments—in short a Jewish answer to Mardi Gras.

Despite their enthusiastic participation in Purim parades and Passover Seders, the traditional Jewish lifestyle has been abandoned by most Israelis. In the coastal towns, many more enjoy the day of rest on the beaches than in the synagogue. Large crowds attend football matches and other sports events.

But some observers believe that the tide is turning and religion is becoming increasingly significant in Israeli life. The Sephardi members of the population have tended to cling more tenaciously to Jewish observance than have their Ashkenazi co-religionists. Coming mainly from North Africa and the Middle East, where piety and poverty tended to go hand in hand, the Sephardi immigrants of the 1950s were a disadvantaged group. Struggling with problems of cultural assimilation and economic deprivation, they had little opportunity to exercise the influence their numbers would justify. But in the 1970s, the government of Prime Minister Menachem Begin made political appointments that gave the Sephardim a greater share of political power. In 1984, the formation of a separate Sephardi religious party—the Shas—broke the Ashkenazi monopoly of the religious establishment. As their influence increased, so did their assertiveness: Sephardic loyalty to traditional Jewish practices and values now makes much greater impact than ever before.

Perhaps in response to these influences, many Ashkenazim are also beginning to reassess the role of Judaism in their lives. The Six Day and Yom Kippur Wars, and the increasing hostility of the outside world to Israel in its unsympathetic role as an occupying power, has driven people to look inwards for historical and biblical roots.

Israel today, therefore, may conceivably be more Jewish than at any other time in its short history. Such, however, is not the view of the very small and electorally insignificant minority of ultra-Orthodox. Nothing will satisfy them short of a society based exclusively upon the Jewish law—and many of them are quite prepared to use violence in order to achieve that end.

In his final Independence Day address as President in 1983, Yitzhak Navon warned of the dangers that could arise from all forms of religious and political intolerance. "The question is not if there will be arguments among us, but if we will know how to conduct them," he said. "The question has become a central factor in our lives, in our ability to sustain democracy and, quite simply, to live with each other."

But contentiousness is not confined simply to the theological sphere. Political issues are also the subject of fierce debate—and none more so than Israel's relations with the Arabs. Indeed, there was bitter internal controversy as a consequence of the government's inability to bring the war in Lebanon to a swift conclusion.

According to the government, the sole object of the invasion—named "Operation Peace for Galilee"—was to clear the massive deployment of PLO arms and men away from Israel's northern border, to which they presented a continuing and mounting threat. At first, most Israelis supported the move, but opinion divided dramatically when the invasion force went on to bombard the PLO strongholds in Beirut itself on the grounds that this was a military necessity if they were to bring the operation to a successful end.

In fact, the PLO eventually agreed to leave the Lebanese capital, but only after the city had been severely bombarded. Mediators, such as the American representative Philip Habib, had made earlier attempts to persuade the PLO to leave Beirut, but to no avail. The relief caused by the PLO departure was soon overshadowed by the shocking news that some 800 PLO fighters and Palestinian refugees had been massacred by members of the right-wing Christian militia forces. An estimated 350,000 Israelis—nearly a tenth of the country's population—took to the streets in protest.

However, there were many Israelis, especially among the Sephardi community, who not only applauded the tough line in Lebanon, but also saw the anti-war protestors as virtual traitors. The ferment culminated in an act of political violence in February 1983, when an assailant hurled a hand grenade into a crowd of anti-government demonstrators who were gathered outside the Prime Minister's office in Jerusalem, killing a 33-year-old reserve paratrooper who had fought in both the Six Day and Yom Kippur Wars.

The attack shocked the public into realizing the consequences of Israel's internal dissensions. Interior Minister Joseph Burg described it as "the gravest of warnings" for the whole Israeli nation. "We must remember," declared President Yitzhak Navon, "that we are one people, with one common destiny, and if, God forbid, our existence should be threatened, we are all in the same boat."

Peace protestors are not the only ones to have suffered at the hands of violent extremists. In 1984, Israelis were shocked to learn of an underground Jewish terrorist group that had been mounting attacks against Arabs living in the territories occupied by Israel during the Six Day War. The group's victims included two West Bank mayors, who were both maimed in car-bomb explosions, and three students, killed in a machine-gun attack on the Islamic College in Hebron.

Israelis were disturbed not only that such an organization existed, but by the list of those accused of taking part. Not all were fringe fanatics. Some were prominent members of Gush Emunim (Bloc of the Faithful), the nationalist religious movement spearheading Jewish settlement on the West Bank. Initially, the Gush Emunim community itself was shocked by the revelation.

Rabbi Moshe Levinger, a spiritual leader of the activists, infuriated most Israelis by claiming that his followers had been forced to take the law into their own hands because of the government's failure to safeguard the West Bank settlements against the PLO. "The arrested," he said, "will yet go down in history as dear boys who worked for the state at a time when it did not do enough on their behalf." Most Israelis rejected this out of hand. In a poll conducted by the Tel Aviv daily, *Ha'aretz* , 60 per cent of those questioned said that the anti-Arab violence was unjustified, though 32 per cent felt that it was "totally justified" or had "a certain justification".

For many Israelis, the problem in the occupied territories is part of the much broader question of how to live in peace. They wonder how Israel's future relations with the Palestinians are to be shaped. A former foreign minister, Abba Eban, has said, "When you think of this situation in the light of Jewish history and the struggle of the Jews for equality of rights and status, the paradox becomes agonizing."

But the paradox is recognized, and the fact that it is debated so widely and with such passion is itself a hopeful sign for the future. Indeed, if it can resolve the political and spiritual contradictions that rend it, Israel may yet realize the high hopes of its founders.

"If I am asked to sum up the whole sense of our purpose as a people and of our State," declared Ben-Gurion, "it is that we shall achieve our aims of peace, justice and the brotherhood of man, not by homily and preaching, but by being ourselves an example in our lives, our government and our conduct. And this we shall achieve only through the alliance of the pioneers of labour and the men of spirit."

ACKNOWLEDGEMENTS

The index for this book was prepared by Vicki Robinson. For their help in the preparation of this volume, the editors wish to thank the following: Mahmoud Abu-Ragabah, Dhahiriya, West Bank; Ben-Gurion University of the Negev, Beersheba, Israel; David Ben-Rafael, Embassy of Israel, London; Mike Brown, London; Alex Burke, Bromley, Kent, England; Richard Cleave, Jerusalem; Jane Curry, London; Mandy Davis, Britain and Israel Public Affairs Committee (BIPAC), London; Dorit Farkash, Kiryat Yam, Israel; Neyla Freeman, London; Benjamin Gil, Ben-Gurion University Foundation, London; Sue Haas, BIPAC, London; Shoshan Haim, Israel Ports Authority, Ashdod, Israel; Zelda Harris, Committee of Concerned Citizens, Netanya, Israel; Rona Hart, Committee of Concerned Citizens, Tel Aviv; Klaus-Otto Hundt, Warwick, England; Kibbutz Ma'Agan Michael, Ma'Agan Michael, Israel; Tommy Lamm, London; Linda Levine, BIPAC, Tel Aviv; Nigel Lillicrap, London; Janet McKenzie, London; Jane Moonman, BIPAC, London; Anton Neumann, BIPAC, London; Robin Olson, London; Matsliah Rafi, Ministry of Tourism, Beersheba, Israel; Deborah Richardson, BIPAC, London; Jonathon Riley-Smith, Egham, Surrey; Faye Schlinsky, Ministry of Tourism, Jerusalem; Barry Shenker, BIPAC, London; Michelle Shinegold, BIPAC, London; Pearl Silver, Jerusalem; Angela Silverman, BIPAC, London; Deborah Thompson, London; The Wiener Library, London.

PICTURE CREDITS

Credits from left to right are separated by semicolons, from top to bottom by dashes.

Cover: Hans Wiesenhofer, Vienna. Front endpaper: Map by Roger Stewart, London. Back endpaper: Digitized image by Creative Data, London.

1, 2: © Flag Research Center, Winchester, Massachusetts. 6–19: Hans Wiesenhofer, Vienna. 10, 12: Digitized images by Creative Data, London. 20: Hans Wiesenhofer, Vienna, except upper right: Richard Nowitz, Jerusalem. 21: Hans Wiesenhofer, Vienna, except top centre: Orde Eliason, London. 23: David Rubinger, Jerusalem. 24, 25: Digitized images by Creative Data, London. 26: Hans Wiesenhofer, Vienna. 28: Klaus-Otto Hundt, Warwick, England. 29–51: Hans Wiesenhofer, Vienna. 52: Courtesy of Staats- und Universitätsbibliothek, Hamburg, photo BPCC/Aldus Archive, London. 53: Courtesy of the Rothschild Miscellany from the Israel Museum, Jerusalem. 54: Illumination from 13th-century Haggadah, BPCC/Aldus Archive, London. 55: Jane Taylor from Sonia Halliday Photographs, Weston Turville, England. 56: Illumination from a French history by William of Tyre, BPCC/Aldus Archive, London. 57: Sonia Halliday Photographs, Weston Turville, England. 58: *The Judgement of Solomon*, a 13th-century miniature from a Hebrew manuscript courtesy of the British Library, London, photo BPCC/Aldus Archive, London; 12th-century manuscript courtesy of the Armenian Cathedral Library, Jerusalem, photo Sonia Halliday Photographs, Weston Turville, England; from *Underground Jerusalem* by Charles Warren, pub. Richard Bentley and Son, London, 1876. 59: *Naphtali* by Marc Chagall, © ADAGP, 1985, photo Sonia Halliday/Laura Lushington from Sonia Halliday Photographs, Weston Turville, England; David Rubinger, Jerusalem (3). 60: BPCC/Aldus Archive, London. 61–62: BPCC/Aldus Archive, London. 63: BPCC/Aldus Archive, London. 65: Popperfoto, London. 66: BPCC/Aldus Archive, London. 67: David Rubinger, Jerusalem. 68–76: Hans Wiesenhofer, Vienna. 78: David Rubinger, Jerusalem. 79–83: Hans Wiesenhofer, Vienna. 84: Digitized image by Creative Data, London. 85: Amos Schliack from Focus, Hamburg. 86, 87: Michael Freeman, London. 87 (inset), 88: Hans Wiesenhofer, Vienna. 89: Mark Karras, London. 90: Hans Wiesenhofer, Vienna. 91: Reg Wilson, London. 92: Digitized image by Creative Data, London. 92–98: Hans Wiesenhofer, Vienna. 98, 99 David Rubinger, Jerusalem. 100–103: Hans Wiesenhofer, Vienna. 104, 105: Amos Schliack from Focus, Hamburg. 106, 107: Hans Wiesenhofer, Vienna. 108: Laura Lushington from Sonia Halliday Photographs, Weston Turville, England. 109–117: Hans Wiesenhofer, Vienna. 118: Richard Nowitz, Jerusalem. 121–125: Hans Wiesenhofer, Vienna. 126, 127: Richard Nowitz, Jerusalem. 128–131: Hans Wiesenhofer, Vienna. 133: David Rubinger, Jerusalem. 134, 135: Hans Wiesenhofer, Vienna. 136: Richard Nowitz, Jerusalem— Hans Wiesenhofer, Vienna. 136, 137: Hans Wiesenhofer, Vienna. 138–143: Hans Wiesenhofer, Vienna. 145: David Rubinger, Jerusalem. 146, 147: Amos Schliack from Focus, Hamburg. 149: David Rubinger, Jerusalem. 150: Orde Eliason, London. 151: Richard Nowitz, Jerusalem. 152–155: Hans Wiesenhofer, Vienna.

BIBLIOGRAPHY

BOOKS

Aamiry, M.A., *Jerusalem. Arab Origin and Heritage*. Longman, London, 1978.

Avi-Yonah, Michael, *The Holy Land*. Thames and Hudson, London, 1972.

Baedeker's Israel. The Automobile Association, United Kingdom and Ireland.

Banks, Lynn Reid, *Letters to my Israeli Sons*. W.H. Allen, London, 1979.

Becker, Jillian, *The PLO*. Weidenfeld & Nicolson, London, 1984.

Bellow, Saul, *To Jerusalem and Back*. Martin Secker & Warburg, London, 1976.

Ben-Gurion, David, ed., *The Jews in their Land*. Aldus Books, London, 1966.

Ben-Rafael, Eliezer, *The Emergence of Ethnicity. Cultural Groups and Social Conflict in Israel*. Greenwood Press, Westport, Connecticut, 1982.

Bermant, Chaim, *Israel*. Thames and Hudson, London, 1967.

Bermant, Chaim, *The Jews*. Weidenfeld & Nicholson, London, 1977.

Capa, Cornell, *Jerusalem, City of Mankind*. Harrap, London, 1974.

Chapman, Alex, *Begin's Israel, Mubarak's Egypt*. W.H. Allen, London, 1983.

Chomsky, Noam, *The Fateful Triangle*. Pluto Press, London, 1983.

Davis, Moshe, and Levy, Isaac, *All About Israel*. Jewish National Fund, London, 1973.

Dayan, Moshe, *Living With The Bible*. Weidenfeld & Nicolson, London, 1978.

Dicks, Brian, *The Israelis, how they live and work*. David & Charles, London, 1975.

Eban, Abba, *My Country, The Story of Modern Israel*. Weidenfeld & Nicholson, London, 1972.

Eban, Abba, *The New Diplomacy*. Weidenfeld & Nicholson, London, 1983.

Elon, Amos, *The Israelis*. Penguin Books, London, 1983.

Fine, Leon, *will the real israel please stand up?*. Pelmas/Massada, Givatayim, Israel, 1980.

Frankel, William, *Israel Observed*. Thames and Hudson, London, 1980.

Gilmour, David, *Dispossessed*. Sidgwick & Jackson, London, 1980.

Good News Bible. Collins/Fount Bible Society, London, 1978.

Guiladi, Yael, *One Jerusalem*. Keter Publishing House, Jerusalem, 1983.

Herzog, Chaim, *The Arab-Israeli Wars*. Arms and Armour Press, London, 1982.

Hollis, Christopher, and Brownrigg, Ronald, *Holy Places*. Frederick A. Praeger, New York, 1969.

Holy Bible. Authorized King James Version, Oxford University Press, Oxford.

Horowitz, David, *The Economics of Israel*. Pergamon Press, London, 1967.

Isaac, Rael Jean, *Party and Politics in Israel*. Longman, New York, 1981.

Israel Pocket Library, Archaeology, 1974; *Education and Science*, 1974; *History*, 1973; *Immigration & Settlement*, 1973; *Geography*, 1973. All Keter Books, Jerusalem.

Johnson, Paul, *Civilizations of the Holy Land*. Weidenfeld & Nicolson, London, 1979.

Katz, Eliahu, and Gurevitch, Michael, *The Secularization of Leisure: Culture and Communication in Israel*. Faber & Faber, London, 1976.

Kaufman, Gerald, *To Build the Promised Land*. Weidenfeld & Nicolson, London, 1973.

Kedourie, Elie, ed., *The Jewish World*. Thames and Hudson, London, 1979.

Kimche, Jon, *The Second Arab Awakening*. Thames and Hudson, London, 1970.

Kollek, Teddy, and Pearlman, Moshe, *Jerusalem, sacred city of mankind: a history of forty centuries*. Weidenfeld & Nicolson, London, 1974.

Laffin, John, *The Arab Mind*. Cassell, London, 1979.

Laffin, John, *The Israeli Mind*. Cassell, London, 1979.

Landay, Jerry M., *Dome of the Rock*. Newsweek, New York, 1972.

Lange, Nicholas de, *Atlas of the Jewish World*. Phaidon, Oxford, 1984.

Lind, Jakov, *The Trip to Jerusalem*. Jonathan Cape, London, 1974.

Meir, Golda, *My Life*. Futura, London, 1982.

Mikes, George, *The Prophet Motive. Israel Today and Tomorrow*. Penguin Books, London, 1971.

Naamani, Israel T., *Israel*. Pall Mall Press, London, 1972.

Orni, Efraim and Efrat, Elisha, *Geography of Israel*. Israel Universities Press, Jerusalem, 1976.

Oz, Amos, *In the Land of Israel*. Flamingo, London, 1983.

Peretz, Don, *The Government and Politics of Israel*. Westview Press, Boulder, Colorado, 1979.

Perowne, Stewart, *Jerusalem & Bethlehem*. Phoenix House, London, 1965.

Prittie, Terence, *Whose Jerusalem?* Frederick Muller, London, 1981.

Rein, Natalie, *Daughters of Rachel. Women in Israel*. Penguin Books, New York, 1980.

Rosenblatt, Roger, *Children of War*. New English Library, London, 1984.

Sachar, Howard M., *A History of Israel*. Basil Blackwell, Oxford, 1977.

Silver, Eric, *Begin; A Biography*. Weidenfeld & Nicolson, London, 1984.

Statistical Abstract of Israel. Central Bureau of Statistics, Jerusalem, No. 35, 1984.

Sykes, Christopher, *Cross Roads to Israel*. Collins, London, 1965.

Thubron, Colin, and the Editors of Time-Life Books, *Jerusalem* (The Great Cities series). Time-Life Books, Amsterdam, 1976.

Time-Life Books, Editors of, *The Israelites* (The Emergence of Man series). Time-Life Books, Amsterdam, 1982.

Weizman, Ezer, *The Battle for Peace*. Bantam Books, Toronto, 1981.

Wilson, Rodney, *The Economies of the Middle East*. Macmillan, London, 1979.

Zohar, Danah, *Israel*. Macdonald Educational, London, 1977.

Zureik, Elia T., *The Palestinians in Israel*. Routledge & Kegan Paul, London, 1979.

PERIODICALS

"An American Presence", *Newsweek*, June 4, 1984.

"Chief Rabbis in Conflict", *Jewish Chronicle*, September 7, 1984.

"Children of War", *Time*, January 11, 1982.

"Dangerous Inroads", *The Jerusalem Post Magazine*, May 3, 1985.

"God on Their Side", *Observer Magazine*, July 22, 1984.

"Mimouna", *The Jerusalem Post Supplement*, April 11, 1985.

Plascov, Avi, "A Palestinian State? Examining the Alternatives", *Adelphi Papers*, The International Institute for Strategic Studies, London, Spring, 1981.

"The names game", *The Jerusalem Post Magazine*, June 22, 1984.

"The Troubled Soul of Israel", *Newsweek*, October 4, 1982.

"The Verdict is Guilty", *Time*, February 21, 1983.

"What Next For Israel?", *Time*, July 9, 1984.

"You're in the Army Now", *SHE*, February, 1985.

INDEX

Page numbers in italics refer to illustrations or illustrated text.

Colour separations by Fotolitomec, S.N.C.
Milan, Italy.
Typesetting by Tradespools Ltd.,
Somerset, England.
Printed and bound by Artes Gráficas
Toledo, S.A., Spain.

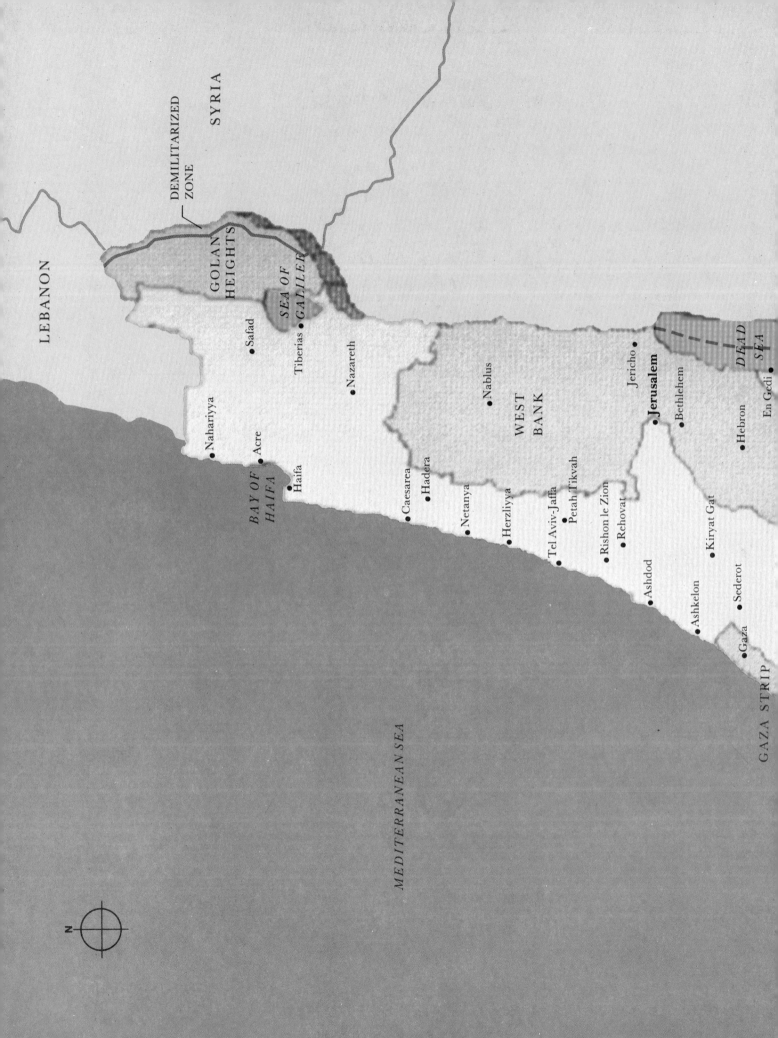